Author
Appreciation

I met Sis Nosi in 2012 when I was 16 years old and in Matric. She interviewed me for the Vision4 Women mentorship programme at a time when my self-confidence and overall outlook on life were poor and negative. Being part of the Vision4 Women mentorship programme helped me discover my vision, strengthened my relationship with God, and dream big for myself. The photos from the Fast Forward graduation kept me motivated and helped lift me from my lows when I was struggling at university.

She introduced me to my first CA (SA) mentor, motivated me when I was failing modules and feeling distraught, and even attended my graduation and 21st birthday party. She opened her home to me, introducing me to her husband and children, transforming our relationship beyond the mentorship programme. Throughout my university years and in my career as a Chartered Accountant, Sis Nosi remained a consistent source of guidance and support.

I highly recommend *The Gift Within* to anyone who enjoys thought-provoking and emotionally charged memoirs. Whether you're a fan of philanthropy or simply appreciate well-crafted stories, this book is a must-read. *The Gift Within* is a testament to Sis Nosi's talent, and the book will stay with you long after you've turned the last page. I am excited for what the book has to offer, and I believe that her legacy will transcend generations through *The Gift Within*.

– Amanda Hobana CA (SA)

The Gift Within could not have been written by any other individual than Nosiphiwo Ncoyo. Through this memoir, she takes us on her life's journey of self-discovery, self-mastery, tenacity, perseverance, resilience, and a purposeful life lived in service of others. The resonant lessons she shares through this book will reorient the reader towards finding their own *raison d'être* (reason for being).

– Dr Bridgette Gasa-Toboti

Nosi inspires me because she is someone who is not afraid to jump, both literally and metaphorically. In *The Gift Within*, she shares her deeply personal story of resilience and how her life experiences – both good and bad – have shaped her to be the incredible woman she is today. This book is more than a memoir.

At its heart, this is a story of how a township girl became a woman of substance and influence, while carrying an enormous heart full of compassion and love for others.

From taking bold leaps in her own entrepreneurial journey, to uplifting countless girls through her Vision4 Women mentoring programme, to being an amazing friend and role model, Nosi's life is a testament to the power of the gifts we all carry within. She has faced adversity with grace, embraced change with open arms, and shown countless women what is possible when you trust your purpose.

I hope *The Gift Within* will be a call to action for anyone standing at the edge of possibility, and give them a glimpse into a future filled with promise. I am sure it will move you, inspire you and, most of all, remind you to embrace the leap.

– Gillian Mc Ainsh

Nosi Ncoyo, known simply to me and many other young mentees as "Sis Nosi", stepped into my life about 11 years ago at the tender and impressionable age of 17, when I had a dream to be a medical doctor. She visited my community in the northern areas of Gelvandale, Port Elizabeth, in order to interview a few eligible candidates at my high school for her Vision4 Women mentorship programme that she founded. Upon meeting her, I was immediately drawn to her kindness, strength, humility, and grace. Her presence was captivating. To me, Nosi Ncoyo quickly became everything I envisioned for myself as an adult or career-driven woman and lady one day.

Sis Nosi always had an open heart before us. She laughed with us, and we cried together in success and struggles – and of course, we always had time to dance!

Nosi Ncoyo, as an author, will always be a most captivating storyteller, who will bravely open her heart to her readers with wisdom and compassion. Her consistently admirable character will no doubt shine through in her writing and penned experiences. As an author, she will have another platform to share her gift with the world, and in doing so, she will most certainly succeed in inspiring many others to do the same.

– Dr Amy Titus

The Gift Within is a powerful testament to the generosity and compassion that define its author. With a heart for giving, she continues to inspire and empower readers to embrace kindness, resilience, and self-discovery. She has walked an incredible journey—one that makes her uniquely qualified to write this book. Her contributions to community development and her role as a conduit for change stem from lived experience. Through her work, she has demonstrated an unwavering passion for uplifting others, fuelled by her deep ability to listen to their stories, see herself in them, and act with empathy and understanding.

This book is not just a reflection of her journey but a continuation of it—an extension of her commitment to community upliftment. She has poured a piece of herself into everything she does, and her passion for helping others has always been evident. Her life has been guided by the intention to do good, and this book serves as the culmination of her purpose: to fulfil God's mandate by touching the lives of ordinary young people who, like her, have faced struggles and dreams alike.

I have no doubt that this book will inspire many.

– Prof Zoleka Soji
Acting Deputy Dean – Faculty of Health Sciences, NMU

THE
GIFT
WITHIN

NOSI NCOYO

THE GIFT WITHIN

HOW EVERY EXPERIENCE SHAPES THE GIFT YOU ARE MEANT TO SHARE

THE GIFT WITHIN
HOW EVERY EXPERIENCE SHAPES THE GIFT YOU ARE MEANT TO SHARE

First Edition, First Imprint 2025
ISBN: 978-0-6398535-9-8
Copyright © Nosi Ncoyo

Editor: Eloise Scoble

Published by: Inspired Publishing
PO Box 82058 | Southdale | 2135 Johannesburg, South Africa
Email: info@inspiredpublishing.co.za | www.inspiredpublishing.co.za

All rights are reserved. Apart from any fair dealing for the purpose of research, criticism or review as permitted under the Copyright Act, no part of this publication may be reproduced, stored in a retrieval system or transmitted, in any form or by any means, electronic, mechanical, photocopying, recording, or otherwise, without the prior written permission of the copyright holder.

This book is dedicated to my late parents,

*Matilda Mnqwazi (Tildas), Nomvuyo Qubenge (Blackie),
Thobile Mali (Toast), Cingelwa Mali (Nowans)*

Contents

Author Appreciation i

Acknowledgements 14

CHAPTER ONE
Whispers Of Goodbye 17

CHAPTER TWO
Sy Lyk Soos Haar Pa 40

CHAPTER THREE
Divided Loyalties 50

CHAPTER FOUR
Nosiphiwo – The Name Foretold 64

CHAPTER FIVE
Bridges Of Sacrifice 80

CHAPTER SIX
A New Beginning In Zwelitsha 97

CHAPTER SEVEN
Faith Found 111

CHAPTER EIGHT
The Panties That Told A Story 124

CHAPTER NINE
Sacred Contradictions.. 143

CHAPTER TEN
The X-Factor 158

CHAPTER ELEVEN
From Admin Desk To Training Room...176

CHAPTER TWELVE
Just Do It 194

CHAPTER THIRTEEN
When The Church Closed It's Doors... 215

CHAPTER FOURTEEN
From Outcast To Advocate.. 233

Acknowledgements

To my husband and X-Factor, Xolisa Ncoyo—I thank God for you. Your love, partnership, and unwavering support are my greatest blessings.

To my sons, Qhama and Phaphama—you have brought immense joy into my life, a true blessing in every way.

To my siblings, Thotyelwa and Phumeza—your unwavering love and support have carried me through life's twists and turns. Thank you for always making me a proud big sister. *Eswekileni forever.*

To my one and only brother, Yamkela—I still cannot speak of you in the past tense. Your life was taken so tragically, but you will forever be in my heart.

To the members of my beloved WhatsApp groups: *Harry and Thethelwa Legacy*—I am because you are. *The Royal Family*—I cherish each and every one of you. *The Real Friends of Jozi*—I always look forward to our time together.

To my glam squad—Zam, Hlehle, and Abby. You are magic. The back cover of this memoir is a testament to that.

To Vision4 Women Family

Gill, Bayanda, Akhona, and Laura—your vision and dedication warm my heart every single day.

Noluthando, Xoli, and Lungi—oh my word, where would I be without you?

Sis Ntuthu and Sis Thozama—you gave the Vision4 girls more than just delicious meals; you gave them your heart.

Destiny Helpers—thank you for always coming back to uplift your little sisters.

Vision4 Women mentors—your love for the girl child is inspiring. Thank you for partnering with me on this journey.

Vision4 Teachers—thank you for introducing me to my girls. Because of you, I am now a mother to over 800 girls.

To my sisterhood and friends of my heart—you know who you are. Thank you for giving me the space to be vulnerable. Your unwavering support through life's changing seasons means the world to me.

To everyone who has loved, supported, and mentioned my name in rooms full of opportunity

Last but not least to my publisher, Darren August—you showed me what's possible. *The Gift Within* could have remained just a dream if not for you instilling a hunger to make it a reality. Thanks to you and your dedicated *Inspired Publishing* team, I can now proudly say: *I am an author.*

Dear Reader—thank you for picking up this book. Whether you were drawn to it by curiosity, a recommendation, or a personal longing for inspiration, I believe it has found you at the right time.

CHAPTER ONE

WHISPERS OF GOODBYE

I tossed and turned, my body sinking into the plush mattress of the five-star hotel bed. Despite the luxurious surroundings, I struggled to fall asleep, my mind racing with thoughts of my mom lying in a hospital bed. The continuous beeping sound on my phone only added to my anxiety, and I couldn't help but keep checking it for any news. Eventually, I must have dozed off because the next thing I knew, the ringing phone jolted me out of my deep sleep. I slowly reached over to pick it up. Looking at the caller ID, I saw an unfamiliar number. My heart sank as I thought it could be the hospital calling about my mother's condition. I hesitated before answering the call, my heart racing with fear. I took a deep breath, mustered all the courage I could, and answered the call. A woman, whom I later learnt was a nurse, was on the line.

Nurse: "This is Dora Nginza Hospital. May I speak to Nosiphiwo Ncoyo?"

I struggled to make sense of her words; my thoughts jumbled and raced. Fear and uncertainty threatened to overwhelm me.

Me: "Speaking."

Nurse: "I am calling you concerning your mother, Nomvuyo."

I couldn't bear to hear what the nurse was about to say over the phone, so I quickly interrupted her. "Please, can you call my husband instead?" I said, my voice shaky and my eyes filled with tears.

Nurse: "But you are the one put here as a contact person."

Me: "I don't want to hear what you are about to say; please call my husband." My voice was sharp and biting as I demanded her to call my husband. I could feel my heart pounding in my chest. I was angry and impatient.

She paused for a moment before agreeing to call my husband. I guess she could sense the tension in the air and knew it was best to act quickly.

Nurse: "What's his number?"

Me: O8..........and I hung up the phone, feeling overwhelmed with emotion.

My mother had fallen sick two months prior, and I remember the day she called me to tell me she had been diagnosed with HIV. I answered the phone and could hear the weakness in her voice. She told me that she needed to tell me something important, and then she revealed that she had been diagnosed with HIV. I could hear the vulnerability in her tone and could sense her fear. "I always had a feeling," she said, "but I was too scared to get tested. I didn't want to know for sure." In the call, she also told me she was afraid of dying and was uncertain about her future.

As we spoke on the phone, my heart was crushed by the weight of the truth I knew but could not bring myself to say. I listened to her while she spoke and feigned surprise and concern, but I knew about her status because her doctor, who was close to both of us at the time, had already confided in me about her HIV-positive status. I had kept the truth buried deep within me. Even though I already knew about her HIV status, the weight of her words hung heavy on my heart as I also had not been sleeping well ever since I received the news. I could feel the tears welling up in my eyes.

When she was about to end the call, she paused and then pleadingly, she whispered, "Promise you won't tell uMama" (we both called my grandmother "mama"). I felt a knot form in my stomach as I understood the weight of her request. I wanted to assure her that everything would be okay, but the lump in my throat prevented me from saying anything. I hesitated for a moment, but I eventually gave in and promised her that I wouldn't say anything. "UMama will only worry," she said. "I don't want to burden her with this." She continued now her voice strained with emotion. "You know how she can be. If we ever have an argument, she'll use this against me." From then on, it became a secret between us, and I carried its weight on my shoulders.

In 2004, South Africa was at the height of a public health crisis and political controversy surrounding HIV/AIDS. The virus had already taken hold, with millions of people infected, but the government's response was marked by denialism and delay. President Thabo Mbeki's administration, influenced by AIDS denialists, questioned the link between HIV and AIDS and resisted rolling out antiretroviral treatment (ARVs) on a national scale. This stance caused widespread confusion and outrage, as it denied people access to life-saving medication.

The Treatment Action Campaign (TAC) was at the forefront of challenging government policies. Activists fought hard to compel the state to provide antiretrovirals through public health facilities. Many hospitals were overwhelmed by HIV-related illnesses such as tuberculosis, and without proper treatment, infections like these turned fatal.

For people living with HIV, 2004 was a time of fear and uncertainty. Stigma surrounded the diagnosis, often leading to isolation and discrimination. There was no standardised protocol for how patients were informed of their results. Counselling services, meant to prepare individuals for their diagnosis, were not always available or adequately implemented. My mother became a victim of this broken system—her diagnosis was not delivered with care or sensitivity but over the phone. No measures were taken to prepare her to receive her diagnosis or to comfort and support her.

I arranged for us to meet urgently, and I remember my mother telling me how worried she was about the stigma surrounding HIV. She feared how people would react and what they would say if they found out about her status. She spoke about the fear of being ostracised and treated differently because of her diagnosis. I felt a pang of sadness and frustration at the thought of my mother carrying this burden alone. I knew that she needed our family's support. I was determined to convince her to open up to my grandmother. I took a deep breath and said, "Sisi (how I called my mom), I know that it's hard, but you don't have to carry this burden alone. Please, tell uMama about your HIV status so that we can all support you."

My mother's eyes welled up with tears as she replied, "I've been thinking about that a lot, and I think it's unfair that she doesn't know; I have decided to tell her. I didn't want to hurt her or make her worry about me." She asked me to accompany her to my grandmother to inform her about her status.

The thought of telling my grandmother about my mother's HIV status was a daunting one. She was not easy to read, and she had never been one to give away her emotions easily. I knew that anticipating her reaction was going to be nerve-wracking.

As we made our way to my grandmother's house, my mind was racing with all the possible scenarios. Would she be angry? Dismissive? Would she refuse to believe it? When we arrived, she greeted us with her usual stern expression. "What brings you here?" she asked, her eyes flickering over to me as it was unusual for me to visit them during the week.

My mother took a deep breath and looked my grandmother straight in the eyes. "Mama," she said, her voice steady. "I need to tell you something." My grandmother's expression didn't change, but I could see a glint of concern in her eyes. "What is it?" she asked, her voice softening just a little.

The room was quiet except for the sound of my mother's voice, trembling as she told my grandmother about her diagnosis. There was a long silence, and I held my breath, waiting for my grandmother's reaction. To my surprise, her expression softened. She reached across the table and took my mother's hand, giving it a reassuring squeeze. "Oh *mnt'anam* (my child), I'm so sorry to hear that. We will get through this together." My mother's eyes filled with tears as she felt the weight of her secret lifting off her shoulders. She knew that she would need her support more than ever when her health began to decline. "It's going to be okay, sisi," I whispered, caressing her back gently. "We're going to support you every step of the way." My mother nodded, her eyes red with tears.

Over the next few minutes, we sat together in a shared embrace, crying and holding each other closely. It was a moment of intense emotion, but it was also a moment of unity and love. At that moment, we knew that no matter what lay ahead, we would face it as a family, with all the strength and support that we could muster. As we eventually pulled away, wiping our tears and taking deep breaths, I felt a sense of gratitude for the love and connection we shared. We were a family, united in our love for each other, and that was something that could never be broken.

You might be wondering what I was doing in a hotel room the night before I received the call from the hospital.

In February 2003, I registered a training consultancy named Vision4 Consulting in Port Elizabeth now known as Gqeberha. When I launched my training consultancy, I was filled with enthusiasm and optimism. Armed with limited experience and a passion for helping people grow, I was eager to share my passion with the world. As a new business owner, I soon realised that building a brand and attracting clients was no easy task. It needed more than passion.

Two years before starting a training consultancy, I opened a hair salon to supplement my income. I called it Lebone Hair Salon and specialised in ethnic hair. It was a venture I had always been interested in, and I felt confident that I could leverage my entrepreneurial skills to make it a success. At first, the salon was a welcome distraction from the challenges of growing a consultancy. I loved interacting with clients and creating a warm and welcoming environment. And as word spread about my salon, I started to see a steady stream of customers. However, running two businesses at once was more difficult than I had anticipated. Between managing schedules, ordering supplies, and marketing my services, I found myself struggling to keep up with the demands of both ventures. I tried to prioritise my time and focus on the areas that needed the most attention, but no matter how much I tried, something always fell through the cracks. As time went on, I began to feel stretched thin and burnt out. I knew that something had to change. I couldn't keep trying to do everything myself, and I didn't want either of my businesses to suffer. That's when I decided to employ my mother to manage the salon.

At first, I was hesitant to ask her. I knew that employing a family member in my business could be a tricky proposition, and I didn't want to create any unnecessary tension or conflict. After a lot of thought and lengthy discussion, my husband and I agreed that employing my mother was the best solution for everyone involved. She had been unemployed for most of her life, so working at the salon was going to be her first "professional" job.

I knew that the decision to employ my mother could potentially change the course of our relationship. Growing up, I didn't have an easy relationship with her. Due to various circumstances, I was raised primarily by my grandmother. My relationship with my mother had mostly been strained, so employing her at the salon could be a chance for us to reconnect and rebuild our relationship. Working together would give us a chance to spend more time together, communicate more openly, and find common ground. And I was right. As my mother took on more responsibility at the salon, our relationship began to shift. We started talking more frequently, and our conversations became more meaningful. We talked about our goals, hopes, and fears. We also discovered that we had more in common than we had realised.

Working together also gave us a chance to build a relationship based on mutual respect and appreciation. I saw firsthand how hard my mother worked to keep the salon running smoothly, and I began to appreciate her and view her in a new light. And I could tell that she was proud of me for building my own business and pursuing my dreams. Having my mother at the hair salon helped me to focus exclusively on my training consultancy.

At the beginning of 2004, I signed contracts for my training consultancy with an organisation that needed me to implement training projects in major cities like Johannesburg, Cape Town, and across the Eastern Cape. My excitement about my business breakthrough was short-lived as it was met with my mom's HIV diagnosis. Her health began to deteriorate. She was at some point admitted to a hospice, but when she was discharged, she was not fit to continue working at the hair salon. She moved between my home and the care of my grandmother and my great aunt Nozipho. On Sunday 30th May, my mother felt seriously ill and had to be admitted to Dora Nginza Hospital, one of the biggest public hospitals in the Eastern Cape, located in Port Elizabeth. On the same day, I had to fly out to Cape Town. My mind was racing as I tried to figure out what to do. On the one hand, my mother needed me, but on the other hand, my clients had paid for my travel and accommodation, and I had learners waiting for me to deliver the session. I had to make a good first impression. I felt torn between my personal and professional obligations. My mother and grandmother pleaded with me to go. I went to visit my mom in the hospital before rushing to the airport.

I walked into my mom's hospital room anxious and my heart pounding. The sterile smell of antiseptic filled my nose as I approached her bed, where she lay still and quiet, her eyes opened as she was looking into space as if in a world of her own.

I took her hand, and she held my grip. One by one, family members started to come in, some with faces showing concern and sadness. The room was filled with a sound of laughter and conversation, mainly complaints about poor service at the hospital. It was comforting for me to know that even if I had to leave for work, I was leaving my mother surrounded by family members who loved her.

Amid the noise and laughter, my mom was just quiet and refused to eat. Looking down at her, I noticed how pale and frail she looked, her once vibrant spirit now subdued. As I sat by her side, she didn't say anything, but her silence spoke volumes. It was as if she knew that her time was running out and that this might be the last time we would see each other. She squeezed my hand weakly, and I felt a lump form in my throat. Her eyes were sunken, revealing her hunger and thirst. I sat by her side, holding her hand, trying to urge her to eat something.

"Sisi, please, you need to eat something. It's not good for you to skip meals," I implored, my voice laced with concern. But my mother just shook her head weakly. "I don't feel like eating anything. I'm just really thirsty, *ndibawela into emuncu* (I'd appreciate something sour). "Can you get me Lemon Twist, please?" she asked, her voice barely audible.

Without hesitation, I jumped out of my chair and headed to the hospital canteen. My heart was thumping as I walked briskly through the corridors; my mind racing with thoughts about my mother's health. When I arrived at the canteen, I could feel my breath coming in quick gasps. As I waited in line waiting for the waiter to serve me, I could feel my anxiety rising. Every second that passed felt like an eternity. I just wanted to get back to my mother's side to give her the drink she had asked for.

Finally, it was my turn at the counter, and I paid for the drink and rushed back to my mother's room. When I got there, she was still lying in bed, staring into space and not participating in the conversation going on in the room except to ask her cousins to lower the noise when they were complaining about the hospital. But as soon as she saw the bottle in my hand, her face lit up with a small smile. "Thank you," she said, her voice barely above a whisper. I opened the bottle, holding it for her and she asked to sip it with a straw, and I could see the relief wash over her face. I stayed by her side for what felt like hours, holding her hand and trying to soak up every moment with her, not knowing that it might be the last.

As I finally stood up to leave, I leaned down, kissed her on her forehead and whispered in her ear: "I love you, sisi." She responded, "I love you too *mntanam*." I had brought her favourite blanket to the hospital. She whispered, "Don't leave the blanket here, take it with you." I said my goodbyes to her and family and with a heavy heart, walked out of the hospital room, tears streaming down my face, feeling as if I had just said goodbye to my world.

As I sat in the car on my way to the airport, I was deeply worried and concerned about my mother. I couldn't help but think about how weak she looked in the hospital bed, and the thought of leaving her there weighed heavily on my mind. My husband, who was driving the car, could sense my anxiety. He reached over and took my hand, squeezing it gently and said, "Don't worry, everything is going to be okay, usisi will be fine." I looked over at him, my eyes filled with tears. "But what if something happens while I'm gone?" I asked, my voice choked with emotion. My husband smiled warmly at me, his eyes filled with love and understanding. "We'll stay in touch, and I'll keep you updated on her condition every step of the way," he said, his voice calm and reassuring. I nodded weakly, feeling comforted by his words.

By the time we reached the airport, I felt a little more at ease. I hugged him tightly, grateful for his unwavering support and love. As I boarded the plane, I was still conflicted about leaving my mother in the hospital and going to work.

As I settled into my seat on the plane, I felt a knot form in my stomach. I knew that I had to focus on my work, but it was hard to shake the feeling that I was abandoning my mother when she needed me most. I tried to push those thoughts aside and concentrate on the task at hand, but they lingered at the back of my mind throughout the entire flight. I tried to distract myself by reading a book, but my mind kept drifting back to her and the hospital. As the plane took off and rose high into the sky, I found myself looking out the window and thinking about my mother. Throughout the flight, I couldn't stop thinking about my mother and wondering how she was doing. When I finally arrived at Cape Town International Airport, I felt a sense of relief and sadness. I was relieved that the flight was over, but I was also sad to be so far away from my mother when she needed me the most.

As I stepped into the grand lobby of the luxurious five-star hotel where I would be staying during my first training contract, I was awed by the sheer opulence and grandeur of the place. The sparkling chandeliers, plush carpets, and ornate furnishings all spoke of the extravagance and indulgence that surrounded me. But despite the obvious luxury of my surroundings, my mind was preoccupied with worry and concern for my mother. Every moment, I found myself thinking about her and her condition in the hospital.

As I made my way to my room, I found myself constantly checking my phone for updates from my family about my mother's health. I couldn't shake off the unease and concern that seemed to follow me everywhere I went. Even as I unpacked my bags and settled into my plush king-sized bed, my mind was still consumed with thoughts of my mother. I tried to distract myself by praying, singing praise and worship songs and begging God to heal my mother.

As I lay down trying to get ready to sleep, I couldn't shake the feeling of unease that had been haunting me ever since I arrived. The soft sheets and fluffy pillows were meant to provide comfort, but instead, they felt like a constant reminder of the distance between me and my mother. The silence of the room only served to amplify my worries and I found myself imagining the worst possible scenarios. The luxurious surroundings that were meant to provide a sense of calm and relaxation only added to my feelings of guilt and anxiety.

After I dropped the call with the nurse, I called my husband to find out what the nurse wanted. He told me that she had asked him to bring fresh clothes to the hospital on the next visit. Relieved, I let out a deep breath. He assured me that everything was fine, but I couldn't shake the sense of unease that had settled over me.

I arrived at the hotel on Sunday night and prepared to facilitate training on Monday morning in the hotel conference room. On Monday, as I stood in front of my training class, trying to focus on the lesson, my mind kept wandering back to my mother. I called relatives to confirm if they had visited her and they assured me they had. However, I later found out that they were not being truthful.

As the day wore on, my anxiety only grew. I tried to distract myself by diving deeper into the training material, and then, suddenly, I blurted out to one of my students, a stranger by the way, "I think my mom has passed on today." The student looked at me, startled, unsure of what to say. I realised then how inappropriate my behaviour was and how unprofessional it was to burden my students with my personal problems. The experience left me feeling ashamed and embarrassed. I knew I needed to find a way to manage my emotions better and keep my personal life separate from my professional one.

As I packed up my materials and said goodbye to the last participants, I felt a weight lift off my shoulders. The training facilitation had been a success, but it had taken its toll on me. My shoulders ached from carrying the burden of responsibility for the group, and my throat was sore from talking all day.

On Tuesday, as I made my way through the airport security line, I couldn't help but feel satisfied. But underneath that feeling, there was a nagging worry that kept me on edge. I clutched my phone tightly in my pocket, checking it every few minutes for updates. The buzz of the airport faded into the background as my thoughts turned to my mother, and I wondered what news the next call would bring.

But as I waited for boarding to begin, my anxiety grew. What if I received the news of her passing while I was on the plane? The flight attendants smiled at me as I boarded the plane, but their cheerful greetings seemed hollow and meaningless. I made my way down the aisle, searching for my seat, my heart was pounding in my chest. As I buckled myself in and adjusted the air vent above me, I couldn't shake the feeling that something was wrong. The plane was filled with the usual sounds of passengers settling in—the rustle of bags being stowed and the click of seat belts being fastened. But to me, it all felt surreal and disconnected.

As the plane took off and soared into the sky, I felt disoriented and uneasy. The world outside the window looked so different from the one I knew—the sky was deep blue, the clouds puffy and white. But none of it made sense to me. Whenever the pilot announced that we were getting closer to our destination, my heart jumped. I couldn't bear the thought of what I might find when I got off the plane. Eventually, the plane touched down in Port Elizabeth. I gathered my belongings and stepped out into the terminal, my heart pounding. I scanned the crowd for my husband's familiar face. Instead, I saw my sister-in-law waving at me with a smile. Confusion flooded my senses, and I quickened my pace to meet her. My heart raced as I approached her, already sensing the worst. "Your husband asked me to pick you up," she said hesitantly, as if unsure how to break the news. "Is everything okay?" I asked, my heart sinking because of the look on her face. "Yes, everything is okay; he is busy at work today." My mind reeled as I tried to process her words. My husband had never asked anyone to pick me up from the airport. Something was wrong. Something was very wrong.

She drove me to my house, her eyes fixed on the road ahead. She tried to make conversation, but I was unresponsive. As we pulled into the driveway, I saw a group of church people gathered inside my house. My husband and some family members were there. I knew something was wrong. They were singing hymns, their voices blending in a mournful chorus. "What's going on?" I asked, my voice trembling. They stopped singing, their faces sombre. "Your mother has passed." One of them said gently. "Why didn't anyone tell me?" I cried out, my heart pounding in my chest. "We thought it would be best if you found out here," another explained. "Your sister-in-law was told not to tell you in the car." I felt a wave of betrayal wash over me as I realised I had been lied to.

Everyone had known the truth all along. The nurse was calling to tell me about my mother's passing and everyone, including my husband, kept it from me. The shock made me feel faint, and I clutched onto one of the church members for support.

We drove in silence from my house to my grandmother's, the weight of grief heavy upon us. When we arrived, I could see that she had already received the news. Her face was swollen with tears, her eyes red-rimmed and puffy. As soon as she saw me, she let out a strangled cry and collapsed onto the floor. I rushed over to her, my own tears blurring my vision. I cradled her in my arms, trying to hold her up. "*Umnt'anam akekho, umnt'anam akekho*" (my only child in gone), she sobbed.

As soon as the words left my grandmother's mouth, it felt as if someone was holding a knife and piercing my heart. The pain was so intense, so sharp that I could barely breathe. Every beat of my heart felt like a reminder of the loss I had just suffered. My mind was a whirlwind of memories, regrets, and unanswered questions. How could she be gone? How could God not save her after I prayed so much begging him? My grandmother's sobs shook her body, and I could feel her heart breaking. I wanted to scream, to rail against the injustice of it all. My mother was gone, and nothing would ever be the same.

As I sat in the living room, surrounded by family and friends, we all tried to come to terms with what had happened. The room was filled with a sombre silence, broken only by the occasional sniffle or sob. Despite the overwhelming grief we all felt, we knew that we had a solemn duty to fulfil. We had to prepare for my mother's funeral. The next few days were a blur of activity. We went to the funeral home to make arrangements and choose her coffin. We wrote an obituary and had to decide on the details of the service itself.

On the day of the funeral, we gathered at the church, dressed in our finest clothes. As I sat on the bench at my mother's funeral, listening to the speakers share their memories and thoughts about her, I couldn't help but feel disappointed. While their words were kind and heartfelt, they didn't seem to capture the essence of who my mother truly was. I couldn't help but feel a sense of bittersweetness. For the better part of my life, my mother and I had been distant and disconnected. We lived in different worlds, with different priorities and different values. It wasn't until the final four years of her life that we found our way back to each other, to bridge the gulf that had separated us for so long. But those four years were precious to me. I saw a warrior in her that I wanted to talk about.

As the service went on, I leaned over to my husband, seated beside me. "I want to say something," I whispered. "I need to pay tribute to my mother." I wasn't part of the programme, but without hesitation, he approached the pastor to make the request. Moments later, I stood at the podium, facing a sea of expectant faces. Taking a deep breath, I began, my voice trembling slightly. "My mother," I said, "was a woman who finished strong." I went on to share stories and memories of my mother, highlighting the qualities that made her so special to me and to those who knew her.

"I didn't always have a close relationship with my mother," I continued, my voice steady but low. I went on to describe how my mother and I had reconnected, and how we had worked to build a relationship despite the many obstacles that had been in our way. I spoke about the conversations we had shared, the moments of laughter and tears, and the way we had found common ground in our love for each other.

As I spoke, I felt the weight of my grief lift, if only for a moment. It was a relief to acknowledge the complexity of our relationship, honouring both the struggles and the ways we had overcome them. When I finished, the room fell into a reverent silence. Then, slowly, people began to rise and applaud. Their response was more than just appreciation; it was an acknowledgement of the courage it took to speak openly about my mother, about our imperfect relationship, and about how love, despite its messiness, remains worth celebrating.

As I stepped away from the podium, a wave of peace washed over me. It wasn't a perfect tribute—far from it. But it was real; it was honest, and it was my way of honouring my mother, even in death.

REFLECTION

Grief does not follow a straight path, it curves, pauses, and sometimes circles back when we least expect it. I have learned that healing is not about forgetting but about carrying love forward in new ways. My mother is no longer here, but she lives on, in the way I speak, in the lessons she left behind, in the warmth of her memory.

There are days when the loss feels fresh, like an old wound reopened. But then there are moments of light, when I hear a church hymn she loved, when I laugh the way she used to, when I look at my body structure or listen to the way I speak and realise how much of her is still with me. And in those moments, I know that love never truly dies.

- What has helped you navigate the pain of losing someone you love?
- How have you found a way to honor their memory and continue to live fully?
- If you could say one last thing to someone you've lost, what would it be?

_____

_____

_____

_____

_____

_____

_____

CHAPTER TWO

SY LYK SOOS HAAR PA

My grandmother raised me. She was my constant, the anchor in a life where my mother drifted in and out like a tide. When my mother had me, she was young, too young to carry the weight of motherhood alone. Her boyfriend's family rejected her, and that wound never seemed to heal. She would disappear for long stretches, leaving me behind with her mother, only to return unexpectedly. Each time she left, I missed her. Each time she came back, I resented her.

I buried my emotions in books. My love for reading began early. I still remember sitting cross-legged on the floor, clutching a copy of *Ityala Lamawele* by S.E.K Mqhayi when I was in Sub-B (Grade Two). It was a high school set book, but I devoured it anyway, page after page, feeling the words stir something inside me. Not long after, I tackled *Buzani Kubawo* by W.K Tamsanqa and the list went on.

At home, my grandmother kept a bookshelf brimming with books. Some were English novels written by James Hadley Chase and Danielle Steel that my grand-uncle, Oompie Ndari, loved to read. "I'm a royal reader," he would say proudly, teasing me whenever I stumbled over unfamiliar words. "You wouldn't understand; your schooling is through Bantu Education." He would chuckle at his own jokes, but I'd push through, determined to understand. Sometimes, I asked him for help, and though he'd boast and joke, he always gave me the answers.

Among the novels on the shelf were first aid books that intrigued me. My grandmother, who worked for Stellenbosch Farmers Winery, was a trained first-aider. Those books were filled with pictures, diagrams of the human body, instructions on how to bandage wounds, and images that explained childbirth in unsettling detail. That's how I discovered the truth that despite what I'd been told, babies don't arrive on airplanes. Whenever I heard footsteps, I'd slam the book shut and shove it back on the shelf. I didn't need to be told that some knowledge wasn't meant for me, not yet.

Our home was a simple four-roomed house, lit by flickering paraffin lamps and candles. We had no electricity, so we cooked using a prima stove. There was a tiny radio that ran on batteries, which were expensive. When they ran out, it took a while to replace them. On rare occasions, the radio worked, my grandmother let me listen to radio plays. I cherished those moments. When the batteries went flat, silence filled the house again, a silence I grew accustomed to.

My grandmother believed in keeping to oneself. "Don't visit other people's houses," she would say sternly, as though other homes held hidden dangers. She disliked people with too many friends and warned me not to be one of them. I played with other kids during the day, but I always made sure I was home before she returned from work.

In the quiet moments, reading became my companion, and stories were the light that banished the darkness. I wrote in a black two-quire book, creating stories I envisaged would one day be performed on Radio Xhosa. That book was my treasure, a journal, though I didn't know the word back then. I poured my dreams onto its pages, plans for a fifteen-room house, prayers to God, and ideas for my future. I still wonder what happened to that book. Those stories, written in a child's scrawl, kept me company in a way no one else could.

Even today, in an age of screens and technology, I keep a two-quire book by my side. It holds my ideas, my plans, and my to-do lists. I'm looking at one right now as I write these words.

One night, under the dim glow of the paraffin lamp, I decided to write about myself a personal profile of sorts. But as I pieced my story together, I realised there were gaps. I needed details only my mother could provide.

She was home that night, sitting on the bed, her arms crossed as if shielding herself from questions. I hesitated but asked anyway.

"*Sisi, ndazalwa ngabani ixesha?*" (What time was I born?)

She looked up sharply. "*Oh, nibuzwa ezozinto esikolweni?*" (Is that what they ask you at school?)

"No," I said softly, "I just want to know."

She dismissed me with a wave, irritation flashing in her eyes. "I'm not going to answer that nonsense."

I persisted, explaining that it wasn't for school; it was for me. But she ignored me, and I knew then that some questions were better left unasked. There was another question I had carried with me for years, buried deep inside. I had overheard whispers on the street, people saying I looked like someone named

Thobile. But after that night, I didn't dare ask my mother anything about my birth or Thobile.

****

My heart pounded as my mother pointed to the ominous house and whispered, "Go inside and ask for Nowandile." Doubt flooded my nine-year-old mind. How could she, my own mother, ask me to set foot in that wretched place? Didn't she know the horrors that transpired within its walls? The echoes of my grandmother's warnings whenever we passed that house resonated in my thoughts, urging me to stay far away from this house of darkness, "*Ungaze usondele kulandlu, kubulawa abantu*" (Don't go near that house; people are killed there). I imagined a place stained with blood. But with fear gripping my small frame, I reluctantly obliged. After all, she was my mother, and disobedience to one's elders had dire consequences. As I took steps toward the entrance, my feet felt weighed down by the stories lingering in the air. Time seemed to slow as I knocked on the door, the hollow sound echoing through the quiet. As I approached the door, I raised my hand and knocked, but there was no answer. I hesitated for a moment, unsure of what to do next, but then noticed that the door was slightly open. I cautiously pushed it open and peered inside, where I saw two men seated at a table, drinking beer and chatting animatedly while music played softly in the background.

My heart was pounding, and I felt a surge of fear as I realised that I was in a stranger's house. But I knew that I had to be brave and find the person I was looking for, so I mustered my courage and spoke up.

"Excuse me," I said, my voice shaking slightly. "I'm looking for Nowandile. My mother told me to come here."

The men looked up at me and one of them gestured towards what appeared to be a bedroom. "She's in there," he said.

Taking a deep breath, I made my way towards the bedroom and knocked gently on the door. To my relief, it opened slightly, revealing a group of people inside.

A woman stood in the doorway, her presence soft but commanding, like sunlight breaking through a cloudy sky. Her inviting smile, soft and genuine, lit up her face, the corners of her eyes creasing with kindness as if she had been waiting just for me. Around her, two girls and a boy played, their laughter filling the air like music, carefree and full of joy.

"I'm looking for Nowandile," I said, my voice barely above a whisper. "My name is Nosiphiwo."

The beautiful woman stepped forward and pulled me into a warm embrace. "*Umntanam*" (my child), she said softly. "You have come at last." Despite the strangeness of the situation, I felt a sense of comfort and belonging in her arms, grateful for her kind and loving welcome.

Proudly and affectionately, she introduced me to the girls before gently lifting me and carrying me towards the house next door.

As we approached, two middle-aged women emerged from within, their eyes scanning me with a mixture of curiosity and hesitation. The woman holding me gestured gracefully, "*NguSa'sendlini lo*," she said, pointing to the larger woman. "*Ngu Gladys lo*," she added, nodding toward the smaller-framed one. "They are your grandmothers."

In that fleeting moment, her voice softened as she muttered something in Afrikaans, unaware that I could understand fragments of it. I was in Standard One after all and Afrikaans had been woven into our curriculum. Her words, "*Sy lyk soos haar pa*," bore a secret truth unveiling the resemblance I bore to a father I had never known.

Nowandile tucked a crisp two rand note into my hand, her touch quick and deliberate, as if she wanted the moment to pass unnoticed. "Come back tomorrow," she said, her voice soft but tinged with something unspoken. I looked down at the note, a small but powerful treasure. Back then, a two rand note wasn't just loose change; it was paper money, smooth, crisp, and folded neatly between your fingers, making you feel like you were holding something valuable. And with it, you could buy a lot too. I carefully tucked it into my pocket and headed toward the soccer field across from my father's house. They called it *Ibala lamaRoma* (the Roman field), named after the popular local soccer club, AmaRoma.

I spotted my mother standing at the edge of the field, her arms crossed, watching the road as if measuring the distance between the present moment and whatever lay behind her. When I reached her, I pulled out the two rand note and handed it over.

She took it without hesitation, folding it in half with a practised motion and slipping it into the pocket of her dress. Her usual soft expression shifted, replaced by something I couldn't quite place, sharp, and serious. Then she leaned closer, her voice low but deliberate. "Don't tell your grandmother or my husband about this. Do you hear me?"

The weight of her words landed like a stone in my chest. I wanted to ask why, why this visit needed to be a secret, but the warning in her eyes stopped me cold. I bit my lip and gave a small nod, the kind that says, "I'll do as you ask, even though I don't understand."

REFLECTION

Some truths find us quietly, long before we're ready to hear them. For years, I'd heard whispers that I looked like a man I never knew. But it wasn't until I stepped into that house and my stepmother quietly said, *"Sy lyk soos haar pa,"* that everything fell into place.

In that moment, I felt both seen and invisible, acknowledged by my appearance, but still a stranger to the man who shared it with me. It was strange to feel like I belonged to something, yet still felt distant.

This moment made me think about identity, family, and truth. Do we truly become ourselves when we uncover hidden parts of our story, or do these truths create new questions? And how do we hold the joy of understanding while also dealing with the pain of what was never given?

- Have you ever experienced a moment when a hidden truth was revealed to you?
- How did it change your perspective or relationships?
- Are there any difficult truths in your life that you have struggled to accept or share?

_____

_____

_____

_____

_____

_____

_____

CHAPTER THREE

DIVIDED LOYALTIES

The first time I met Bell-Bell (Bheza), I was just a little girl, about six years old. My mother, with that soft smile she wore whenever she was around him, introduced him as "uBhuti," I later learnt that he was her boyfriend. He seemed okay to me—short, handsome, and light-skinned. But I overheard the whispers between grown-ups, warning my mother about him. "That man will ruin your life," I once heard my aunt hiss when they thought I wasn't listening. And later, when I saw her face swollen and her arm in a plaster cast, I knew those whispers weren't just gossip; they were warnings my mother refused to heed.

My mother decided to marry Bheza without consulting her family. She spent the night away with him and woke up a *makoti* (a bride), stepping into a new life without their blessing.

Thereafter, we moved into a shack in Khiwane, part of Soweto-on-Sea. I called him "Bhuti" as I called my mother "Sisi", and he was the only one bringing money home. Every Friday, he'd bring his wages, and no matter what else went on, there was always food on the table. I never went to bed hungry. My mom, though jobless, kept our shack spotless. The wooden walls were lined with newspaper wallpaper, the shiny silver prima stove sat polished with Brasso, and even the enamel water bucket gleamed. It was so clean inside, you'd forget it was a shack until it rained and the roof betrayed us with its endless leaks.

My mother enrolled me at eMzomncane Lower Primary School for Sub-A (Grade One) in 1982. The school was just a short walking distance from our shack, but I hated it. I hated that the other kids' uniforms looked sharp and proper, while all I had was a maroon-and-white jersey, knitted by our neighbour. The wool felt rough against my skin, the stitches loose and uneven, and the difference was painfully obvious. I also owned a maroon-and-white stitched knitted balaclava and would pair these with my brown corduroy pants. I stood out, but not in the way I wanted.

Lunchtime was worse. My classmates would open their lunch boxes to reveal sandwiches stuffed with polony or cheese, sometimes both. I unwrapped leftovers from last night's dinner, samp, cabbage, or stew and the teasing would start almost immediately. Peanut butter sandwiches from the school's feeding programme became my salvation, though I'd still toss my packed lunch on the way home so my mother wouldn't know I hadn't eaten it.

Then there were birthdays, theirs, never mine. Kids from well-off families brought cakes and snacks for the entire class, and teachers gushed over them, calling their parents by their first names. I sat quietly watching, wishing for just one day like theirs. I never told anyone how much it hurt. I only wiped my nose whenever the green mucus appeared, hating the teacher's sharp rebuke: "Wipe your nose! You look disgusting."

Despite all that, I found solace in excelling at school. I stayed in the top three, eager for any recognition from teachers. Volunteering for every errand became my way of standing out, and sometimes it worked. But one day, my teacher gave me an ultimatum: no more corduroy pants or handmade jerseys. I begged my mother for proper school clothes, but she could only offer an apologetic smile. "I'm trying, my child. I'm really trying."

One morning, I couldn't take it anymore. Instead of walking to school, I turned back, feeling the weight of shame press down on me. But my escape was short-lived. My mother found me, grabbed my hand without a word, and dragged me all the way to school. In front of the other kids, she gave me a sharp slap that stung more than just my cheek it stung my pride.

I only wore a real school uniform when the junior choir needed me for a competition. I had earned a place as one of the lead singers, and for that moment, the teachers found me a borrowed uniform. I loved going to Sisonke Community Hall for those choir competitions. I felt like a different person in those clothes, as though I belonged, if only for a day.

Later, Bhuti bought a house in Zwide on Mtati Street, just a few kilometres from Khiwane and about nine kilometres from my grandmother's house in KwaZakhele, where I was born. This house felt like an upgrade, a four-roomed structure made of bricks, a far cry from the shack I'd known. For the first time, we didn't have to queue with neighbours at a shared communal tap. Instead, we shared a tap with our back neighbours. And we had a toilet that flushed, unlike the bucket system I was accustomed to.

Bhuti's mother, MamCirha whom I called Makhulu, moved in with us, bringing her sister and two of her sister's grown children. Bhuti's younger brother, Wiseman, came too, and he was the only one I connected with. The others, though, brought chaos. Weekends were a haze of drinking. Makhulu and her sister would lounge on their beds, passing zol back and forth, their voices thick with smoke and slurred from alcohol. Their arguments, sharp and mean, filled the room late into the night.

I had no choice but to sleep with them in the same room. Every night, I climbed into the bed I shared with MamCirha, squeezing myself at the bottom near her feet. It was cramped and uncomfortable, the blankets smelling faintly of tobacco and spilt liquor. The air in the room felt suffocating, thick with the scent of burnt herbs and stale breath.

The tension in the house was always simmering, ready to explode. Bhuti was short-tempered, and when arguments broke out between him and the others, it was as if a storm had rolled in. His rage was familiar; it was the same fury he unleashed on my mother during their fights. The shouting, the slammed doors, and the bitter silence afterwards became the rhythm of our days.

One Saturday, my mother and I made our way to Korsten for groceries. Korsten was, and still is, one of the busiest areas in Port Elizabeth. Known for its lively markets, discount stores, and bustling streets, it was where people from different neighbourhoods came to stock up on essentials. Korsten wasn't glamorous, but it had everything—fresh produce stalls, butcheries, second-hand shops, and street vendors calling out their specials.

For many, Korsten was a lifeline, especially for families trying to stretch every rand. Its gritty energy reflected the survival spirit of the community where people navigated both struggle and opportunity side by side. It wasn't just a place to shop; it was where stories were exchanged, secrets traded, and old friends unexpectedly reunited.

That day, as we walked through the crowded streets, dodging taxis and squeezing past throngs of people, my mother and I felt lighter. We laughed, enjoying the freedom that came from leaving our tense home life behind, if only for a few hours. But, like the unpredictable streets of Korsten, life at home could shift without warning.

The mood shifted as soon as we returned home. The moment we stepped inside, Bhuti called me into the bedroom.

"Who did your mother talk to in town?" he demanded, his voice laced with suspicion. His eyes bore into mine, and I felt my heart begin to race.

"No one," I whispered, truthfully.

"Are you sure?" he pressed, his tone darker now, filled with accusation.

I shook my head, insisting that she hadn't spoken to anyone. But before I could register what was happening, his hand struck my face with a force that echoed in the room.

"Liar," he spat, the venom in his voice cutting deeper than the slap. "Just like your mother."

At that moment, I learnt the harsh truth: some things were better left unspoken. Later, when my mother warned me, "Don't tell Bhuti you visited Nowandile's house," I understood the weight of her words. Silence wasn't just a shield; it was our survival strategy.

Growing up, I moved between homes. Whenever the fights between my mother and Bhuti became too much to bear, she would pack our bags without a word and take me to my grandmother's house in KwaZakhele also called eBesuthwini. It became a pattern, our escape route from the storms at home. During school holidays I stayed with my grandmother, who left for work early each morning, leaving me alone until she returned in the evening. I quickly learnt to navigate the quiet hours, filling the time however I could, waiting for the sound of her footsteps at dusk.

It was one September holiday when Sisi and I were on our way to my grandmother's house, following the familiar route through streets I knew by heart. But that day, something shifted. Without warning, Sisi took an unexpected detour and stopped in front of that dreaded house. Pointing toward it, she said almost casually, as if it were nothing, "Go inside and ask for Nowandile." I didn't realise it at the time, but that small shift in direction would change everything. It was the beginning of a revelation that would shake the foundations of what I thought I knew about myself and my family.

The day after my first encounter with Nowandile, I returned to her house to honour her invitation. My grandmother was away at work, and Sisi had gone back to her marital home. I slipped into this new world with ease, joining the two young girls and the boy, who by now were no longer strangers. We were on a first-name basis—Thotyelwa and Phumeza, my sisters, and Bhasi, our cousin, Glady's son.

We spent the day lost in the joy of childhood, our laughter filling the yard like music. We raced across the concrete paving, darted behind an old, rusting car, and chased each other through endless rounds of hide-and-seek.

As I was looking for a place to hide, I saw a man carrying two cases of beer. When our eyes met, he put down the cases and I saw tears in his eyes. I was scared and confused by his behaviour, so I quickly ran away to find my sisters. After what seemed like only a few minutes, Nowandile called me inside the house.

As I stepped inside the house, I found the man I had seen earlier, still sitting there, eyes red from tears. Unsure of what to say, I greeted him, "*Molo, bhuti.*"

He looked at me for a long moment, then shook his head. "I'm not *bhuti*," he said, his voice soft but firm. "I'm your father, Thobile."

The name rang in my head like a bell, echoing through years of whispers and glances from relatives and neighbours. It was the man they always said I looked like. I didn't know what to feel, excitement or confusion.

It was getting late, and I needed to get back to my grandmother's house. Before I could leave, he pressed a crisp ten rand note into my hand. "Come back soon," he said with a smile.

I clenched the money tightly in my hand, my heart pounding. Ten rands was a fortune in 1984. If my mom could buy tripe and vegetables from Chithibhunga's Cash and Carry with just two rands, I could only imagine what this could buy. However, excitement wasn't what I felt; fear crept in instead. My mother's voice echoed in my mind, stern and clear: *"Don't tell your grandmother you went to Nowandile's house."* What would I say if Mama found the money? I even thought about throwing it away just to avoid trouble.

Despite my fear of getting caught, I figured out ways to slip away unnoticed and found myself drawn back to my father's house. It wasn't hard, my grandmother thought I was with my mother, and Bhuti thought I was at my grandmother's. My father's house sat on Salamntu Road, halfway between Mama's house in eBesuthwini and Bheza's place in Mtati Street.

His house wasn't like my grandmother's quiet home. This one buzzed with life. Electricity hummed through bright lights, and a large, colourful TV lit up the room. I marvelled at it back at home;

the neighbours had a tiny black-and-white set. People crowded around it, paying five cents to watch. But here, at Tata's house, I could watch whatever I wanted, movies and music videos without anyone charging a cent.

I slipped between homes without ever packing a bag I didn't need to. My father's wife, Nowandile, insisted I call her *Mama*, and Tata embraced me as if I'd always belonged. Neither asked if I had permission to visit. Instead, they welcomed me with open arms. By the end of my September holiday, I left their house with bags full of clothes. When I got back to Bhuti's house, he didn't even notice. He assumed the clothes were gifts from my grandmother.

Tata's house had everything a child could dream of and life at his house was nothing like the quiet orderly life at my grandmother's. Thobile owned a tavern called by his nickname "Toast" that buzzed with people at all hours. He had been a boxer once and now ran a boxing promotion company, training new fighters and producing a few professionals. Money was never a problem. There was always enough for outings to the beach, Playland, and Happy Valley. But the house was full, and it wasn't always easy to tell who family was and who wasn't. It seemed as if anyone could drift in and stay for a while.

What stunned me the most was how close I had been to him all along. Tata's tavern sat just a stone's throw from my school,

Emzomncane Primary School, separated only by a boundary wall. All those years he had been right there, on the other side, without me knowing. The nearness of it all felt surreal as if the truth had been hiding in plain sight, waiting for the right moment to reveal itself.

My grandmother had been right about the place. It had a reputation. People whispered about the tavern, "Toast's Slagpan," saying that it was where soccer rivals fought and some never made it home. My cousins, from my mother's side, soon noticed the new clothes and money I had at my disposal. They started following me to Thobile's house on the condition that they would keep the secret. Nowandile welcomed them, letting them sleep over as long as they were my relatives.

The secret visits continued through the December holidays. But one morning, as my cousin Nokuzola was mopping the kitchen floor, we heard a commotion outside. Before we could figure out what was happening, the door burst open, and there stood Makazi Nawe, Nokuzola's mother. She didn't say a word but just stormed in, grabbed Nokuzola by the arm, and slapped her hard across the face. The sound echoed through the house. "Let's go," she barked, dragging Nokuzola out the door without a second glance. I froze, fear wrapping around me like a cold blanket. Makazi Nawe was my grandmother's younger sister. If she knew we were here, it was only a matter of time before

Mama found out too. I had no idea who had tipped her off, but the secret was out, and I knew there would be consequences.

Soon after, a series of family meetings followed. The elders gathered, their voices rising in anger and betrayal. My grandmother and the rest of the family felt deeply hurt by my mother. "How could Nomvuyo take the child to that house?" they demanded. "After everything that boy and his mother did to this family?"

Sisi blamed me. She had no idea that I had gone back to Thobile's house without her knowledge. I don't know what she expected me to do after that first visit with Nowandile. But what I do know is that my visits to Thobile's house only deepened the cracks already forming in Sisi's marriage to Bheza. Whether those visits were the cause of their separation, or whether it was infidelity, emotional abuse, or violence that finally tore them apart, I'll never know for sure.

REFLECTION

Growing up, I found myself trapped between two worlds my mother's family, where I sought love and belonging and my father's family, where I was searching for a connection despite their denial of me.

Each visit to my father's house felt like an act of rebellion, a secret that I had to keep hidden from the people who raised me, especially my grandmother. I kept these visits from her, afraid of the judgment I might face for seeking a connection with the man who had not been a part of my life. In those moments, I carried the weight of divided loyalties, on one side, my mother's family, who had supported me through the years on the other, my father's family, who I longed to understand despite their rejection. I didn't know how to balance the love and respect I had for both sides without feeling torn apart.

Reflecting on this, I see how these experiences shaped my understanding of loyalty and identity. I learned that we can love and honour multiple people in our lives without betraying who we are. Today, I understand the importance of being open about the complexities of relationships and allowing space for honest conversations, even when loyalty feels divided.

DIVIDED LOYALTIES

- Have you ever felt caught between two people or groups you care about?
- How did you handle it, and what did you learn from the experience?

_____

_____

_____

_____

_____

_____

_____

_____

_____

CHAPTER FOUR

NOSIPHIWO – THE NAME FORETOLD

After that family meeting, the warnings were sharp and clear, I was never to visit my father again. Yet, the ache to see my sisters, my dad, and Nowandile gnawed at me. But it wasn't meant to be. Around that time, I noticed my mother started drinking heavily. Her marriage to Bheza was over, and she moved back in with me and my grandmother, but only intermittently. This time, her return brought nothing but conflict. The house, once filled with quiet routine, became a battleground as she fought with my grandmother over the smallest things.

Rumours reached me that my father and Nowandile missed me too. They had several meetings with my grandmother, trying to work out a way to keep me in their lives. To my surprise, my grandmother took an instant liking to Nowandile. It didn't take long before trust was built between them, and my grandmother, perhaps worn down by my mother's absence and chaos, agreed to let me stay with Nowandile and Toast. The idea of someone else taking care of me, especially while she worked, was a relief.

The arrangement was simple: I would live with them when I started Standard Two and visit my grandmother now and then since their house was only about three kilometres away. I could hardly believe it, after all the secrecy and sneaking around, I was finally going to stay with my siblings full-time. Even better, the school was right next door to my father's house, so no more long walks.

It felt as if life had been turned upside down in the best possible way. At school, my dignity was restored. Gone were the days of worn-out shoes and mismatched hand-me-downs. Now, I had a full school uniform, brand new shoes, and a lunchbox filled with sandwiches stacked high with polony and cheese or, even better, Kentucky Fried Chicken on Mondays.

It was our family ritual to pile into my dad's bakkie on Sundays and head to Commercial Road, where Port Elizabeth's KFC stood like a beacon of excitement. My father would order a bucket of chicken, and we'd each pick out our own drinks and desserts. I always went for the trifle, the sweet layers of sponge cake, custard, and jelly felt like the perfect end to the weekend.

Sitting at the back of the bakkie with my siblings, giggling and sipping on my soda, I felt something unfamiliar yet wonderful, belonging. School became different too. No longer the kid with corduroy pants, I walked into class with my head held high. I didn't have to explain myself anymore.

You might be wondering why I only met my father when I was nine years old. One day, during one of my mother's visits to my grandmother's house, she asked me to touch my forehead and look for a faint scar. Until then, I had never really noticed it. I never liked my forehead, kids teased me endlessly about it, calling me "Grootkop" (Big Head) and "Jomo Sono," after the football legend with a prominent forehead. These nicknames weighed heavily on me, making me feel ashamed of my appearance.

That day, after I traced the scar with my fingers, my mother giggled and told me a story I'll never forget.

Before I tell you the story, let me start by painting a picture of where my mother comes from.

My mom, Nomvuyo, grew up an only child, raised by my grandmother, Matilda, whose Xhosa name was Notazi (Tazi in short) and her stepfather Wandile Mankayi. But she wasn't born an only child. She had a twin brother, Luvuyo, also called Whitey. My mother, being the darker twin, was affectionately called Blackie, a nickname she carried throughout her life. In our township, many knew her as "Mambaza," after the popular South African male choral group Ladysmith Black Mambazo which sang in the local vocal styles of *isicathamiya*.

Matilda had been married before to Sandi Qubenge, and they had five children, four of whom tragically passed away young. My mother never knew her father or any of her siblings, including her twin brother Luvuyo, who died when they were just months old. Wandile, who had raised my mother since she was a little girl, was the only father she ever knew. He never treated her as a stepchild, and she even took his surname, Mankayi and clan name, Qwathi. Wandile and Matilda had no children of their own, so my mother was their pride and joy.

My mother was surrounded by the love of her aunts and uncles, who cherished her as the last living child of their sister. My grandmother was the eldest daughter in her family, and everyone called her Sisi or Maka Blackie out of respect. They spoilt Nomvuyo endlessly, perhaps because she represented a piece of the nephews and nieces they had lost.

Although Matilda was the second-born child to Harry and Thethelwa Mnqwazi, her elder brother vanished without a trace at an early age (*watshipha*), forcing her into the role of the eldest. She had to take on responsibilities typically reserved for boys. My grandmother would often boast, *"Mna ndandisolusa, ndibetha iintonga namakhwenkwe"* (I herded livestock with the boys, wielding sticks like them).

It's no wonder she was called Nogqwashu behind her back by family and neighbours. While beautiful, she wore a stern expression, one that said, "Don't mess with me." Matilda's siblings all played a vital role in our lives. Her sister, Florence Nongemkile, whom we lovingly called Mha, was the family's nurturer, a true mother hen to all her nieces, nephews, and grandchildren. Mha lived on John Knox Bokwe Street in Zwide Township, and at some point, almost every family member stayed at her home. People often said my mother looked more like Mha's daughter than her niece, with both of them sharing the same dark skin tone and generous spirit. Mha was known for her balance, tough when necessary but incredibly kind. She had six children with the Yumata family, Sipho, Zamile, Fezeka affectionately known as Novi, Sthembiso, Nomalady, and Lumka. My mom was particularly close to her cousin Fezeka, and they grew up like siblings.

Matilda's brother, Zenith whom we called Oompie Zenithi, was quite a character. During a good portion of my childhood, he was in and out of prison, mostly for being part of a syndicate dealing in dagga (marijuana). Back then, the use of dagga was illegal in South Africa, and Oompie's escapades were the stuff of legend. Whenever he returned from prison, he had grand stories to tell, delivered in perfect English. He always had a newspaper tucked under his arm, regardless of how outdated it was. His sisters tried in vain to steer him away from trouble, but prison remained a recurring chapter in his life. His children, Mbokothwana, Mandisa, and Visa, grew up without him.

My grandmother's other sister, Satyiswa, known to us as "Makazi uSatyiswa," often stayed with us because of her rocky marriage to Tekuteku. She had a son, Velile, before she married him, and Velile was a prominent soccer player in his day. Then there were the Ndulula children she had with Tekuteku—Gufi, Xolile, Nonkosazana, Cwete, Nkululeko, and Nkosomzi, all of whom were close to my mom.

Then came Makazi Nawe (full name Naniwe), who married into the Deliwe family. She had two daughters, Noxolo and Nokuzola, who were much younger than my mother and grew up with me. To this day, I still argue with them and Lumka, Mha's last-born daughter, as they insist I call them "*makazi*" (aunt). We grew up playing together, and it feels strange to address them so formally.

My grandmother's brother, Sipho, whom we affectionately called Oompie Ndari, often stayed with us when his marriage to Aunt Nopheza hit rough patches. His children, Danile, Mncedisi,

Wandile, Thembisa, and Thembela, were regulars at our home, and I especially recall the close bond I had with Thembela, who was just a year younger than me. Oompie Ndari was much like his older brother Zenith; both shared a love for reading and were rarely seen without a newspaper tucked under their arm.

Finally, the youngest of my grandmother's siblings is Makazi Nozipho, who never had children of her own but raised Velile's children when he passed.

Our great-grandmother, Thethelwa Mooi, was also a constant in our lives. Her house at Ten Demist Street, Zwide township, was a gathering place for all the grandchildren. To this day, Makazi Nozipho still lives in that ancestral home, holding onto the family's legacy.

My mother, Nomvuyo, never knew much about her biological father Sandi or the Qubenge family until later in her life. Matilda had high hopes for her daughter, dreams fuelled by the opportunities she never had. As a young girl, Matilda left school to care for her father's livestock. From those humble beginnings, she worked as a domestic worker, became a hotel cook and later worked at Stellenbosch Farmers Winery in different positions.

They lived comfortably in their home in eBesuthwini, KwaZakhele. Matilda and Wandile, her husband, had full-time jobs and ran a small business on the side, driving out to farms and nearby towns on weekends to stock up on vegetables. Their

Datsun, a rare sight in the neighbourhood, would rattle its way home, loaded with produce for their thriving community shop. Unlike many families around them, they openly showed affection. Wandile called Matilda *sthandwa* (my love), and their love was something to be envied.

She poured everything into her daughter. Nomvuyo had everything: full school uniforms, pretty clothes her friends secretly borrowed, and the kind of life Matilda believed would keep her from trouble. But Matilda's love came with walls, literal ones. A high boundary wall enclosed their house, keeping neighbours out and Nomvuyo in.

But behind the walls, Matilda ruled with an iron hand. She was meticulous, a perfectionist who could make floor polish from candles and paraffin if need be. She was also relentless in her discipline.

Nomvuyo wasn't free. One day, a close friend of hers overstayed her welcome, and when Matilda came home, she chased the girl all the way home and then beat Nomvuyo for daring to host company. From then on, that friend only met Nomvuyo at school. The walls of their house weren't just physical; they were emotional too. It wasn't long before Nomvuyo felt closer to her stepfather Wandile and her aunts, especially Mha, than she ever did to her mother.

When she lost her house keys one day when she was fourteen years old, the fear of Matilda's wrath drove her to the brink of suicide. Wandile saved her by calming both the storm in her heart and the one in Matilda's.

At school, teachers adored her, and her peers loved her. She was so neat and respectful that the principal of Aaron Gqadu Senior Primary School nicknamed her "Queenie." She may not have excelled academically, but her netball skills made her stand out. But Queenie was not the only popular student. There was also Thobile Mali, athletically gifted and top of his class. Girls flocked to him, and it was only a matter of time before he and my mother noticed each other. Thobile's family lived nearby, and his mother, Nomhle, worked with Matilda at Stellenbosch Farmers Winery. However, the two women didn't get along. Nomhle, with her light complexion and delicate beauty, carried an air of superiority, which rubbed Matilda the wrong way.

When both sets of parents were away for work, Queenie and Thobile took advantage of the empty homes. His sisters never questioned the presence of their brother's secret guest, nor did they tell.

Then, the unthinkable happened. Nomvuyo, at just sixteen, was pregnant.

Matilda was devastated. It wasn't just the pregnancy; it was who the father was. Her colleague's son. A colleague she never liked.

Fueled by fury, Matilda banished her daughter to her grandmother Thethelwa's house on Demist Road, Zwide. But Wandile intervened, insisting that the two families meet to discuss the matter.

The day of the meeting arrived, and Nomvuyo, shamed and scared, was dragged along. Thobile sat quietly as the elders questioned him.

"Do you know this girl?" they asked.

"Yes," Thobile admitted, his voice barely audible.

"Did you sleep with her? Do you know she's pregnant?"

Before Thobile could answer, Nomhle cut in sharply, "Impossible! My son is still in school. He couldn't have impregnated this girl."

Her words stung like slaps. The room erupted into heated arguments, voices overlapping with anger and disbelief. Finally, Nomhle dismissed the accusations with a cold, "*Siyakubona emntaneni*" (We will see when the child is born).

Wandile stormed out, swearing never to set foot in that house again. Matilda was beside herself with rage, her anger fuelled by rumours circulating at work. Whispers claimed that her daughter had lied about the baby's paternity, and Matilda was convinced Nomhle had spread the gossip. Determined to prove she could care for both her daughter and her unborn grandchild, Matilda doubled down. Despite the scandal, she held her head high, but the shame and gossip cut deep. Neighbours warned their daughters to stay away from Blackie, fearing she would spoil them.

My mother withdrew from the world, finding solace only in her aunts, uncles, and cousins. Without their support, she might have lost her mind.

The pregnancy, however, wasn't easy. Her morning sickness turned into something far worse; her health deteriorated significantly. Her feet swelled, and she could barely walk. There was talk of ending the pregnancy to save her life. Doctors had no answers. Matilda, ever the fighter, tried everything, from medical interventions to the prayers of prophets and faith healers. One healer stood out among the rest. She prophesied that the baby would live. "It will be a girl," she said. "She will do great things."

It was during those uncertain months that my name, Nosiphiwo, meaning "with gift" was chosen. There was a long-standing debate between my grandmother and my mother regarding who gave me the name. My grandmother insists it was her idea, inspired by a prophet's words. My mother, however, claims the prophet herself bestowed the name upon me. Regardless of who named me, there is one thing they both agree on: they knew I was a girl long before I was born, at a time when ultrasounds were unheard of. I choose to believe my grandmother's version after all; she is the one who raised me.

I arrived late, on 24 May 1975, after keeping my mother waiting for ten long months. Ten. Not the usual nine. By then, exhaustion had wrapped itself around her like a heavy coat, and when the contractions finally came, her struggle had only begun. At Livingstone Hospital in Korsten, my mother lay in agony, her body refusing to cooperate with the natural course of things.

The doctors tried everything, and in their haste, they reached for the forceps. Cold, metallic hands gripped me as they pulled me into the world. One slip, one small mistake, left a deep scar on my forehead, an unintended mark of entry, etched onto me from the very start.

While my mother lay weak and hurting, the hospital's walls seemed to offer no mercy. Nurses were rough with their words, their sharp tongues piercing deeper than her physical wounds. "*Ingene ilibhanana, ngoku iphuma ilipayina,*" they muttered cruelly, mocking her pain and helplessness. They viewed her cries for help as complaints, expecting her to care for me while she was fragile.

She was forced to lift herself from the hospital bed, each movement a struggle, to bathe me in the cold, sterile bathroom. On shaky legs, she carried me toward the basin, hands trembling from weakness. The world spun as she tried to balance me in her arms, exhaustion dulling her senses. At one point, I slipped, her worst fear unfolding in slow motion. Just as I was about to crash on the hard tiles below, a nurse sprang into action, catching me in the nick of time.

Later, when my mother told me this story, there was awe and disbelief in her voice. She would say, "*Hayi, wawufuna ukuphila nyani, ntombazana.*" (You really wanted to live, my girl). Her words stayed with me because they were more than a remark. They felt like a blessing. From that day forward, the scar on my forehead became more than just a mark. It became a reminder: I was born fighting to survive.

The time for the second visit to Thobile's house came when I was just a few months old. My mother often tells me I was light-skinned, with a striking resemblance to Nomhle. Unfortunately, that second meeting didn't go any better than the first. There was no agreement on how Thobile would take responsibility for me, and his mother remained as dismissive as before. Eventually, my mother's family gave up trying, and my grandparents took on the role of raising me without any support from Thobile's side.

I was born Nosiphiwo Mankayi, and my clan name was MamQwati, honouring my step-grandfather. Growing up, I believed my mother was my older sister. From a young age, I was taught to call her "Sisi," while my grandmother became "Mama," and my grandfather was "Tata." The Xhosa saying "*Akukho mntwana unomntwana*" (a child cannot have a child) shaped this arrangement.

Before my grandparents divorced, they provided everything I needed, ensuring I was always well-dressed. Neighbours often commented on how stylish I looked. If there had been a contest for a best-dressed child, I'm certain I would have won. As the first grandchild on my maternal side, I was the pride of the family. My uncles and aunts adored me, each treating me like their own. If I wasn't on Nomalady's back, I was perched high on the shoulders of Zamile or Velile. Even now, I know without a doubt that my maternal family would go to any lengths to protect me.

REFLECTION

This chapter unveils the deep and painful yet powerful beginnings of my life. It is a story of rejection and acceptance, of struggle and survival. My mother's journey as a teenage mother, caught between the denial of my paternity and the unwavering support of her own family, speaks to the resilience that I unknowingly inherited.

The scar on my forehead is more than a mark left by forceps, it is a symbol of my fight to exist. My mother's near-collapse after birth and the nurse's timely intervention reinforce the idea that my life was meant to be. Even before medical scans, a spiritual healer foretold my existence, my gender, and my name, Nosiphiwo- *With Gift*. This name was not just an identity but a declaration of purpose, reminding me that my life was intentional, valuable, and destined for something greater.

Names carry weight, history, and destiny. They can be a reflection of our past, a declaration of who we are, or a whisper of who we are becoming. Just as my name was given with meaning, we all have the power to define what our existence represents.

As you reflect on this chapter, consider the name you were given

- What does your name mean, and how has it shaped your identity?
- If you could rename yourself based on your life's journey, what name would you choose?

_____

_____

_____

_____

_____

_____

_____

_____

_____

_____

CHAPTER FIVE

BRIDGES OF SACRIFICE

At about five years old, I didn't fully understand what was happening, but I could sense it: Cracks started emerging in my grandparents' marriage and widened like fault lines. Whispers floated in the air, loaded with allegations of infidelity. The story, as muddled as my young mind could grasp, involved my grandfather and one of the neighbour's cousins.

My grandparents' fights weren't quiet things. The house became a battlefield, words like knives slicing through the silence, and fists occasionally following. I didn't just witness the war; I became collateral. My cousin Nokuzola never lets me forget a particular memory: "*Ngumama ubetha utata*" (It's *mama* hitting *tata*), she'd giggle, mimicking my small voice. I had said it innocently when the police were called during one of their blowouts.

I must have caught a glimpse of my grandmother, fierce and unyielding, in the heat of a scuffle, raising her hand against my grandfather. Matilda was tough, tougher than any storm that blew through that house. And when it all crumbled, it was she who remained standing. They fought bitterly over the house, but in the end, it was hers. My grandfather packed his things and left, but not without lingering shadows of affection.

He married again, moved on to his new house, and though his life had changed, he never let go of us. I remember visiting him at his house. He greeted us as if nothing had ever broken. "You're still my children," he'd say, a trace of warmth in his voice, even though the family had fractured long ago. He kept calling us his children, right up until the day he passed.

Life changed dramatically for my grandmother. The woman who had always been strong became grumpy and bitter. With some of their assets halved after separation, she had to start over. She struggled to juggle her job and care for me, often leaving me with relatives and neighbours. Her relationship with my mother, Sisi, turned from bad to worse. It was around this time that my mother started dating Bheza, often disappearing for long stretches.

When my mother returned, the house would erupt in arguments. Matilda would shout at Sisi for not helping to take care of me, and their fights, filled with hurt and disappointment, echoed throughout our home.

After having me, my mother never returned to school and struggled to maintain stable employment. She often faced challenges with her temper, which frequently led to conflicts at work. Though she would find jobs as a general worker in various restaurants, she would lose them in a short space of time, often due to altercations with supervisors or colleagues.

My grandmother carried the weight of our household almost single-handedly on her meagre income from her job at Stellenbosch Farmers Winery. She not only provided for her household, but she also took on the responsibility of caring for my mother and raising me. This added burden often weighed heavily on her, reflecting the challenges we faced as a family.

Every morning at 5:30, my grandmother left the house. She never waited for the sun or good weather. Whether it was raining or freezing, she would wrap her scarf tighter, tuck her handbag under her arm, and start walking. The distance from our home in KwaZakhele to Struandale, where she worked, was five kilometres. She walked ten kilometres daily.

She worked for her employer for twenty-four years. In all that time, she was never late, not even once. She never called in sick, not even when the weather was harsh or when her body begged for rest. She left every morning with the same focus, carrying more than just a handbag. She carried the weight of my future on her shoulders.

When I was much older and driving, I started to see what walking that distance really meant. It wasn't just a journey to her job. It was a sacrifice, a daily promise she made without saying a word. Each step she took was for me so that I could grow up with opportunities she didn't have.

For my grandmother, the decision to entrust my care to my father and his wife was nothing short of monumental. It represented a sacrifice that weighed heavily on her heart, for she had already lost so much. Her four children, each a piece of her soul, had been taken from her, along with the dreams she had nurtured for their futures. Two failed marriages —first to my mother's biological father, Sandi Qubenge and later to Wandile Mankayi— left her with scars that ran deep, while her dignity seemed to dissolve like mist in the morning sun.

But the loss that pierced her the most was that of her only daughter, whose absence left a void that echoed through the halls of her life. My grandmother had envisioned a different path for her, a path filled with education, achievement, and the promise of a brighter tomorrow. Yet, as life often unfolds in ways we least expect, those dreams remained just that: dreams unfulfilled.

****

Staying with my father and his family wasn't without its challenges. In 1985, Port Elizabeth, like many other townships in South Africa, was caught in a storm of political resistance and brutal state repression. Apartheid had reached its boiling point, and every day felt like a tug of war between survival and the dream of freedom. People in the township lived under constant surveillance and tension, as ordinary routines like going to school or buying groceries could quickly turn into moments of terror.

Police patrols were relentless, and police presence came with an unmistakable sense of dread. Armoured vehicles known as hippos prowled the streets, with armed soldiers peering out, ready to unleash violence at the slightest hint of resistance. Tear gas became a familiar scent in the air. It was one of the state's most effective and cruel weapons to disperse crowds. Its sting burnt our eyes and throats as protests and boycotts swept through the townships. We learnt to use wet cloths over our faces, hoping to block the choking fumes.

Schools were at the centre of this turmoil. Students were no longer just learners; they were activists, part of a generation determined to end apartheid. Boycotts of schools and shops were common. Students refused to attend classes under the apartheid education system, rejecting a curriculum designed to keep them subservient. Businesses that refused to support the anti-apartheid struggle were boycotted, creating deep divisions even within the community. In homes, families whispered about politics, knowing that loose talk could mean arrest or worse.

It wasn't just the physical environment that changed; apartheid fractured township life from the inside out. Suspicion became second nature. Anyone could be an informer, paid by the regime to report on neighbours or political meetings. Families were divided by fear and ideological loyalties.

One of the most terrifying aspects of township life during the struggle against apartheid was the use of the "necklace" as a brutal form of punishment. The necklace, a burning tyre filled with petrol placed around a person's neck, became a symbol of violent justice. It was used to deal with people accused of being police informers, traitors, or collaborators with the apartheid regime.

To understand the horror of the necklace, you must first understand the context of those times. Apartheid thrived on division, and the government infiltrated black communities, using bribery or intimidation to recruit informers, known as *impimpis*. These informers would secretly report on political meetings, protests, or individuals involved in the resistance. As a result, activists were arrested, tortured, or killed, and hard-fought plans to overthrow the regime were undone from within.

The need to root out informers grew more desperate as the struggle intensified. Trust became a rare and fragile thing, and suspicion lurked in every corner of township life. When someone was suspected of being an *impimpi*, they were often subjected to swift and brutal street justice. The black communities felt they couldn't afford to wait for trials or legal processes that didn't protect them. The necklace became a grim tool of people's courts, where those suspected of betrayal were tried, sentenced, and executed in front of angry crowds.

I was too young to witness one first-hand, but the stories haunted me. People would describe how the accused were dragged into open fields or street corners, surrounded by a mob chanting liberation songs. Once the tyre was forced over the person's head and doused in petrol, a match would be struck and tossed on the person. The person would scream and thrash as the fire engulfed them, but the crowd, hardened by rage and betrayal, often showed no mercy. The necklace was not just a punishment, it was meant to send a message.

This brutal practice exposed the complexity of the liberation struggle. While the fight was for freedom, not all actions taken in its name were just. Fear, anger, and desperation drove people to do unspeakable things. The necklace became a stain on the anti-apartheid movement, revealing how the line between justice and vengeance could blur.

Yet, it also spoke to the deep betrayal felt by communities, whose survival depended on solidarity. To be an *impimpi* was not just about giving information to the enemy; it was a betrayal of the very people fighting for your freedom. In those times, betrayal carried the highest price, and forgiveness was often a luxury no one could afford. My dad used to say the necklace wasn't just for *impimpis*. The police had their own way of using it, turning their brutality against anyone who stood in their way, especially at night when darkness gave them cover.

Back then, the police harassed us in our house and people in the tavern. The township buzzed with raids. Hippos and police vans rumbled through the streets daily, stopping at our place as if on a schedule. Tear gas canisters became a familiar sight, smashing through windows, and choking us and the patrons in a cloud of toxic fumes. We were just kids, but we knew the drill: soak a cloth in water, cover your nose and mouth, and wait it out. It was terrifying, but it became routine.

One night, everything changed. The police came pounding at the door long after midnight and dragged my father from his bed. We woke up to shouting and commotion, and through the chaos, we watched helplessly as they forced him outside into the cold night, across the road to the open field opposite our house. They weren't there for questions; they were there for punishment. They wrapped a tyre around his neck, the stench of petrol thick in the air. "Where is the gun?" They demanded, their faces twisted with rage. My father didn't own a gun, but in their eyes, every black man with influence had to be hiding something. The flames were only a match away, and they wanted him to confess; whether the gun existed didn't matter.

He denied it repeatedly, standing his ground, knowing that each refusal pushed him closer to the blaze. But when he realised they weren't bluffing and he was moments from being burnt alive, he made a desperate choice. He lied. "It's in the tavern; that's where I hid it," he told them. He hoped this story would buy him a chance. It was a gamble. He knew that once they dragged him back there, the tavern's crowded, noisy environment might give him the split second he needed to disappear.

And it worked. They dragged him across the street to the tavern, shoving him inside as they prepared to search the place. But my father had no intention of waiting for them to discover the lie. As soon as he was inside, he disappeared into the crowd of patrons, slipping through the back door into the night. By the time the police realised what had happened, he was long gone, swallowed up by the chaos of the tavern and the shadows beyond it.

For a long time after, my father was skeptical when people said the charred bodies found in the streets were always those of *impimpis*, informers who had been punished by the community. He knew firsthand that the police, too, used the necklace to kill, to silence, and to terrify. The blackened remains we saw in the mornings weren't always the result of political justice; they were sometimes the cruel handiwork of a regime bent on breaking us, one flame at a time.

The fight against apartheid wasn't just between the people and the government; it also created tensions within the liberation movement itself. Two key groups, the Azanian People's Organisation (AZAPO) and the United Democratic Front (UDF), both wanted freedom from apartheid but had different ideas about how that freedom should look. These differences often turned violent, causing deep divisions within black communities.

AZAPO believed in Black Consciousness, an ideology that emphasised self-reliance, black pride, and the rejection of white involvement in the struggle. Inspired by Steve Biko, AZAPO believed that freedom could only come from black people liberating themselves. They were suspicious of alliances with white activists and called for economic control to be placed firmly in the hands of black South Africans.

On the other hand, the UDF represented a broad coalition of organisations, including civic groups, churches, unions, and student movements. They believed in building unity across racial lines, working together with all South Africans, blacks, whites, and Indians who opposed apartheid. UDF members were often aligned with the African National Congress (ANC) and saw mass mobilisation, such as strikes, protests, and boycotts, as the way forward.

In townships like ours, the rivalry between AZAPO and the UDF supporters often escalated into violent confrontations. Houses were burnt, meetings disrupted, and people loyal to one faction were sometimes attacked by the other.

My father wasn't a politician, but as one of the prominent businessmen in the area, his influence stretched beyond business. He quietly supported anti-apartheid political activities, a choice that placed our household in dangerous proximity to conflict. My father's support for the UDF made him a marked man, creating enemies beyond the oppressive regime.

The threats that our house would be petrol-bombed started quietly at first as whispers in the township. At home, we felt the tension in the air, a weight pressing down on every conversation.

One day, my sisters and I were packed off to stay with Nowandile's relatives in Madolo Street in Zwide.

It was supposed to be a temporary place to keep us safe until things calmed down. We settled into the unfamiliar rhythm of life in Madolo Street, close enough to school at Emzomncane Primary that our routine didn't change much. But at night, fear lingered. Even as children, we knew the danger wasn't over.

Then it happened. Late one night, while my father and Nowandile were asleep, the sound of shattering glass tore through the quiet. Flames erupted outside as a petrol bomb exploded, and chaos filled the air.

When Nowandile told me the story years later, she admitted how terror had swallowed her whole that night. "I was so scared," she said, "I crawled under the bed and prayed they wouldn't come inside." For what felt like hours, she stayed hidden, heart pounding, listening to the crack of windows breaking and the hiss of flames licking at the walls.

Thankfully, the fire didn't spread, and no one was hurt. But the house, our home, was left scarred, with shattered windows and the smell of smoke that lingered long after the flames were gone.

We stayed in Madolo Street for months after that, trying to build some sense of normalcy out of the broken pieces. At least the school run was manageable. Emzomncane Primary wasn't far, and soon we made friends with our many cousins and neighbours.

Madolo Street came alive every afternoon, filled with the sounds of children's laughter. In the township, we didn't need fancy toys to enjoy ourselves; our happiness came from simple, indigenous games that kept us entertained until the sun set low on the horizon. We played games such as *uPuca*, a game of quick hands and precision. Using small stones, we would throw one into the air and try to scoop as many others from the ground as possible before catching the airborne one. It was a test of speed, focus, and friendly competition. The winner always celebrated with a little victory dance, teasing the rest of us.

Hopscotch, or uSkhoji as some of us called it, was one of the simplest but most exciting games we played on the streets of Madolo. All we needed was a piece of chalk or a sharp stone to draw the grid on the ground boxes numbered from one to nine and a small stone or bottle cap to act as the marker.

The rules were easy. You tossed your marker into the first box, making sure it landed neatly inside without touching the edges. Then, on one leg, you hopped your way through the grid, skipping the square with the marker. On your way back, you bent down still balancing on one foot and picked up your marker. If you stepped on a line or lost your balance, it was the next person's turn.

Each round became harder as the marker had to be thrown into the next number. By the time you reached the higher numbers, everyone was watching eagerly, waiting for you to stumble or celebrate your victory. If you made it all the way, you earned the right to "claim" a square by drawing your initials on it. That square would become your rest spot; no one else could step on it during their turn.

It wasn't just a game; it was a social ritual. The older kids taught the younger ones how to balance and play by the rules, while the cheekier ones bent the rules to their advantage, making everyone laugh. We played until the chalk lines faded, or the call for supper interrupted the fun. *USkhoji* taught us coordination, patience, and a bit of strategy.

And in a township life full of disruptions, those small moments of play gave us a sense of control and joy, one hop at a time.

Even though Nowandile and my dad didn't stay with us, they visited often, always arriving with smiles and bags brimming with treats, sweets, biscuits, chocolates, chips, and KFC. Their visits brought warmth and comfort, reminding us that even in uncertain times, we weren't alone.

For a while, Madolo Street felt like home. We grew used to the lively afternoons, the company of cousins, and the familiar rhythm of the neighbourhood. But as the trouble finally subsided and the tensions surrounding my dad began to ease, it was time to return home.

REFLECTION

Sacrifice is one of the greatest acts of love, often unseen yet deeply felt. As I reflect on the sacrifices made for me by my grandmother, my father, and even my stepmother I see how their selflessness built the bridge that carried me forward. My grandmother's decision to let me live with my father, despite her pain, was an act of love that changed my life. It taught me that true sacrifice is not about loss but about creating opportunities for those we love.

Through the years, I have come to understand that sacrifice is rarely easy, yet it has the power to transform lives, mend broken relationships, and create unexpected bonds. It is in those moments of giving whether through time, comfort, or difficult choices that love and strength reveal their deepest meaning.

Now, I invite you to take a moment to reflect on the role of sacrifice in your own life.

- Think about a time when someone else made a sacrifice for you, what did this act of sacrifice teach you about the strength and love of others?
- How did it affect your relationship with that person, and how can you show your appreciation for their sacrifice?

_____

_____

_____

_____

_____

_____

_____

CHAPTER SIX

A NEW BEGINNING IN ZWELITSHA: CHANGE AND IDENTITY

My father was a strategist by nature and a true entrepreneur at heart. He had a way of approaching everything like a well-thought-out business deal, even when it came to family matters. One thing that never sat right with him was the fact that one of his daughters, me, carried the Mankayi surname, while my sisters proudly bore his surname, Mali, and his clan name, Gqwashu. To him, it was more than just a name; it was identity, legacy, and belonging.

But he knew this wasn't a conversation he could navigate lightly, especially with my grandmother. She had already sacrificed a lot by allowing me to live with him, considering the complicated history between them. The topic of a name change was a landmine, and he trod carefully. He tried bringing it up with my mother, hoping she could help sway things in his favour.

My mother, however, knew her limits. She understood that when it came to matters involving me, her word held little weight. She was in and out of my life, while my grandmother had been a constant, unwavering presence steady as a rock, the true guardian of my upbringing. Whatever decisions were to be made, they were not hers to make.

In Xhosa culture, a child born out of wedlock belongs to the mother's family, and my grandmother, not my parents, was the one who held that right over my name. For my father, this was a hard pill to swallow. He was my biological father, after all. But in our world, biology didn't always dictate who you belonged to. Tradition did. And in this case, tradition had the final word.

But my father had a way of waiting for just the right moment, and that moment arrived unexpectedly. He had made a promise to my grandmother to take care of me for the rest of my life, knowing that he hadn't been there for my formative years and never paid damages. With the school boycotts raging, only children in the lower grades, Sub A to Standard Two (grades one to four) were still going to class. Everyone else stayed at home. My father, with his sharp foresight, feared what could happen if I fell behind in school. He had seen what happened to other children during those turbulent years. Some never returned to school, some got into trouble, and others ended up pregnant.

He had big dreams for me, and so did my grandmother. And then, just like that, the opportunity presented itself.

My father's mother, Nomhle, had roots in Adelaide but later moved to Zwelitsha, a township outside King William's Town. The family had long ties there, and my father was a familiar face among their relatives, where her family still lived. It was a place my dad knew well as he was a regular visitor, and relatives from Zwelitsha often came to our home. I still remember meeting them, Gladys and Sa'sendlini, on one of their visits when I first met Nowandile. They were Nomhle's youngest sisters, and they had come from Zwelitsha.

One evening, my father approached my grandmother, laying out his strategy. In 1986, he proposed sending me to Zwelitsha, away from the chaos, to continue my education. I could stay with his relatives there and enrol in Standard Three (Grade Five) at Zwelitsha Higher Primary School. "It's for her future," he insisted, painting a picture of opportunity, a life uninterrupted by politics.

My grandmother listened, her face thoughtful but guarded. There was no room for carelessness, sending me off without raising suspicion would require careful planning. If the neighbours, especially those from eBesuthwini, suspected anything, they could accuse her of selling out to the homeland government. And in that climate, accusations could easily lead to a petrol-soaked tyre and a violent death.

But my father was prepared for every angle. "They've already accepted that she stays with me," he said, reassuring her. "She only visits you during the holidays. Her absence won't raise questions." Still, there was one more hurdle, L.L. Sebe, the head of the Ciskei homeland, was strict about admissions. He didn't want learners from the Republic of South Africa filling his schools. My father explained that to get me into Zwelitsha Higher Primary, he would have to change my surname to Mali, his surname. One of the teachers at the school, Mr. Mali, was supposedly a cousin of his. The plan was simple, I would enrol under the pretense that I was Mr. Mali's daughter.

My grandmother's hesitation hung in the air, but the promise of a better future for me outweighed her doubts. Reluctantly, she agreed. The name change was arranged, and everything fell into place.

It wasn't until much later that I learnt the full truth. Yes, there was a Mr. Mali teaching at Zwelitsha Higher Primary, but he wasn't related to my father. In fact, the connection between them was thin at best. Mr. Mali was just a friend of my father's uncle, Mr.

Minya, the man whose house would eventually become my home. But by then, the name on my school records was already Mali, and the future my father envisioned for me was set in motion.

Growing up, I moved from house to house, each one with its own way of life. In every home, I had to figure out where I fitted in. I became good at reading the room, watching people's moods, listening carefully, and adjusting to what was expected of me. It was a survival skill, but it also shaped how I saw myself. I often felt like a visitor, never really settling or belonging.

Amid all this instability, my grandmother's house was my anchor, my sanctuary. There, I wasn't just another face in the crowd or an extra mouth to feed. I was the only one, the centre of her world. Her love was unwavering, her attention undivided. In her home, I didn't have to compete for space or affection. I could simply be. I can still remember the aroma of her food, the sound of her voice, and the routines that gave me comfort.

This constant movement shaped me in ways both profound and subtle. On the positive side, it made me resilient. I learnt to adapt quickly, to find my footing in unfamiliar situations, and to connect with people from all walks of life. It gave me a unique perspective, and an ability to see the world through multiple lenses. But it also left me with a lingering sense of rootlessness, a fear of attachment that sometimes made it hard to fully invest in relationships. I often wondered if I would ever find a place where I truly belonged, or if I would always be searching for that feeling I only ever found at my grandmother's house.

I was anxious about moving to Zwelitsha. The thought of starting a new school was overwhelming. I remember crying and begging my father not to take me there. My sisters would tease me, saying I would become an "*imboza*" (someone coming from the rural areas to the city) with an accent like our cousin Bhasi. Even though their teasing hurt, I knew I had to go along with it.

My journey began with a 250-kilometre drive to Zwelitsha, where my father introduced me to his relatives in Zone Eight. Among them was his aunt, Nofenishala, who lived with her husband, Fezile, and their children and granddaughter, Nomveliso. I felt an instant connection upon arriving, especially when I spotted Nofenishala's daughter, Nomasomi. I had fond memories of her visit to Port Elizabeth, and seeing her familiar face gave me a sense of comfort in this new place.

My father made sure I was ready for this new chapter. He bought me a brand-new school uniform, stationery, and textbooks, all essential tools for my education. On my first day, he drove me to school, and then returned to Port Elizabeth, leaving me to navigate this new world on my own. It was quite a trek from Zone Eight to Zone Seven, where Zwelitsha Higher Primary School was located, but Nofenishala arranged for me to walk with other kids from the neighbourhood.

As we strolled together, I quickly discovered that they, like me, were not from Zwelitsha. Ntombomzi and Zuko hailed from Cradock, while Siphokazi and her brother, Mbulelo, came from Port Elizabeth. They stayed with their grandmother whom we called "Ncinci." All relocated to Zwelitsha due to school boycotts, and it was reassuring to find friends who understood the circumstances that brought us here. I was delighted to learn that Ntombomzi and Zuko were in my class, and we quickly became inseparable companions both in school and after hours.

My late start to the term, however, came with its challenges. There was much administrative work to be done behind the scenes, including a surname change and the necessity of concealing the truth: I was Mr. Mali's daughter, a secret that allowed me to secure a place at the school. By the time February rolled around and I entered the classroom, the other students were already familiar with each other. Thankfully, my growing friendship with the Mguzulwas helped me acclimate quickly.

It wasn't long before I caught the attention of my class teacher, Mrs. Diko. She noticed my eagerness to learn and how quickly I grasped new concepts. I distinctly remember overhearing a conversation between her and my dad's uncle, Mr. Minya, where she expressed her pride in me for excelling despite starting late.

Being in Mrs. Diko's class felt like a balm for my past wounds. I finally felt seen and valued. I began to thrive in the supportive atmosphere she created, relishing the moments when I was called to the principal's office, not to be punished, but to be recognised for my achievements.

I blossomed academically, consistently ranking at the top of my class every term. I cherished the first seat in the front row, a testament to my hard work and dedication. What once felt like a long, burdensome walk to school transformed into a journey I enjoyed, full of promise and hope.

Moving to Zwelitsha felt like stepping into another world. In Port Elizabeth, the air was thick with defiance. Here, freedom wasn't something people fought for.

Life in Zwelitsha was a world away from what I had known in Port Elizabeth. Back home, the air was thick with defiance. Struggle songs drifted through the streets, and whispered plans of protest carried the hope of a future unshackled from white supremacy. But Zwelitsha had a different rhythm, one that confused me. Here, people spoke of freedom, but not the kind I was used to. It was something they talked about and celebrated every year on 4 December at Bisho Stadium, the day of Ciskei's independence.

I still remember the excitement in my cousins Nosipho's and Mandla's voices when they invited me to Bisho Stadium. "You'll love it," they said. "Free food! Music! Celebrations!" But as much as I wanted to feel the joy they promised, even as a young girl, I could sense something was off. It didn't feel like the freedom I knew we were fighting for in Port Elizabeth. People here didn't seem free. There was a strange reverence for Lennox L. Sebe. Sebe was a prominent political figure in the former Ciskei, a Bantustan (a nominally independent homeland for the Xhosa people) established by the apartheid government of South Africa. He served as the president of Ciskei from 1973 until 1990. Sebe was known for his authoritarian leadership style and his close alignment with the apartheid regime, which granted Ciskei nominal independence in 1981, though it was never internationally recognised.

His name carried weight everywhere I went—like the wind, always present, brushing against every conversation. In my eyes, he had the same tight grip over people that the police in Port Elizabeth did, only now he was draped in admiration.

Nofenishala and Fezile, my Zwelitsha guardians, practically worshipped him. Their pride showed in the way they pointed at their tidy four-roomed house or mentioned their street-sweeping jobs as if they were badges of honour. The salaries were small, but stability was a treasure. They believed they owed that stability to Sebe, and in their eyes, his rule wasn't oppressive; it was salvation.

I knew better than to repeat the jokes I'd heard whispered by the bolder kids in the street because a joke about Sebe wasn't just a joke. Repeating them could earn you more than just a scolding; it could land you in serious trouble. One afternoon, I learnt just how serious those rules were. Sebe's voice crackled through the radio, filling the house with its deliberate, commanding tone. I made the mistake of continuing my conversation.

"Shhh!" Nofenishala hissed, shooting me a sharp look that could cut through steel. *"Quiet! Tata is speaking."*

The room went still. Every sound, every movement came to a halt, as if the air itself held its breath out of respect. At that moment, I understood: When Sebe spoke, the world in Zwelitsha stopped.

I was the teacher's pet, and that came with a price. It wasn't long before I had haters, learners who couldn't wait to settle their grudges with me. But our principal, known affectionately by his clan name, Hlathi, loathed bullying. Every assembly, he'd have us recite after him, *"Inyama ayiyityi enye inyama"* (meat does not eat another meat). It was forbidden to lay a hand on another learner on school grounds, but after school? That's where grudges simmered until the last day of term, the day of reckoning. When someone whispered, *"Ndizakuvala ngawe"* (I'll get you on the last day of school), the dread of that promise lingered in the air for weeks.

It wasn't just my good grades that made me a target. My accent set me apart too. You could be Xhosa and from the Eastern Cape, yet sound worlds apart depending on where you were from. I was from Port Elizabeth, and that alone painted me as "different" from some. My crisp city accent, coupled with my top marks, convinced a few girls that I thought too highly of myself. I didn't, but that didn't matter. They hated me for it anyway.

The last day of school arrived, and the girl who'd promised to "get me" was ready. She and her friends shadowed me as I walked home, their steps in sync with mine all the way from Zone Seven to the grassy patch near Buffalo River, which separated Zone Eight from Zone Nine. She didn't waste any time, hurling insults as her friends cheered her on. I tried to keep walking, hoping to avoid the inevitable fight while in my school uniform, but there was no escape. They had me cornered.

And then, I snapped. "*Ungandiqheli mna, utsho ngokuba ngathi uyikati etshe icala!*" (Don't you dare look at me like a cat that's only been burnt on one side), I spat.

Laughter erupted from the crowd, and I could see the rage flare in her eyes. Before I knew it, we were on the ground, locked in a tussle, her fists raining down on me.

At that moment, a memory jolted through me. I was in Grade One again, bawling after a girl had beaten me up. My mother grabbed my hand, marched me back to the girl, and said, "Fight again. I'm going to beat whoever loses." That girl wiped the floor with me, and when it was over, my mother beat me too, for losing. Since that day, I vowed never to lose another fight.

As the bully from Zwelitsha pinned me down, the memory of my mother's punishment burnt in my mind. I fought back with a fury that startled even me. In no time, I had flipped her over, and with every hit, the cheers of the crowd faded. When it was over, she lay defeated, and I stood victorious, my chest heaving with the effort.

From that day on, no one ever dared to bully me again. I was no longer just the clever girl from the big city. Now, I was the girl who could take you down too.

REFLECTION

As I settled into life in Zwelitsha, I found myself caught between two worlds, the politically charged defiance of Port Elizabeth and the quiet submission of my new surroundings. I was no longer just a child navigating school, I was a young person trying to understand the weight of authority, belonging, and identity.

Being seen by Mrs. Diko gave me a newfound sense of recognition, yet changing my surname felt like a loss of something deeply personal. Experiencing bullying and school fights toughened me, but it also made me question what it meant to stand up for myself. And in the presence of LL Sebe's rule, I realised how different people respond to leadership, some with loyalty, others with resistance.

Through all these experiences, I learned that adapting to change is not just about survival, it's about understanding who you are in new and unfamiliar spaces. It's about recognising what you hold onto and what you let go of.

Take a moment to reflect on your own experiences. Think about the moments in your life where change forced you to grow, and where leadership good or bad left a lasting impact. Consider the questions below as you explore your own journey.

- How do you adapt when faced with new environments, people, or situations?
- Can you identify any moments where you overcame initial discomfort to embrace a new chapter in your life?
- How do you respond to different types of leadership, do you challenge, follow, or find a middle ground?

_____

_____

_____

_____

_____

_____

_____

_____

CHAPTER SEVEN

FAITH FOUND

After school, Zwelitsha buzzed with life, much like the vibrant streets of Madolo. Despite the many activities filling the afternoons, three women stood out, though the only name I clearly remember is Sis Mpumie. These women were much older than us, but they had a passion for youth development. Their dedication reminded me of my grandmother back in eBesuthwini, who also poured her heart into uplifting young people around her.

After finishing our homework, we'd head straight to Sis Mpumie's house, where something exciting was always happening. Her home became the hub of extra-curricular activities, from gumboot dancing to rehearsing for plays. One of the most anticipated events was the Miss Zwelitsha competition. We practised for weeks, honing our performances and preparing to compete against other youths from the neighbourhood.

I never made the cut for Miss Zwelitsha, though my friend Siphokazi Mguzulwa did, carrying our hopes and excitement with her. But it was the acting that truly captivated me. I threw myself into every role, finding joy and purpose on stage. With every play we performed, my passion for storytelling deepened. For a while, I even believed that acting would be my future. Those afternoons at Sis Mpumie's weren't just about fun and competition, they shaped my dreams and nurtured the seeds of creativity within me.

During school breaks back in Port Elizabeth, I made it a point to gather the youth of eBesuthwini, teaching them the plays and songs that Sis Mpumie and her friends had introduced to me. I remember scrawling in my black two-quire notebook, "One day, I will have a drama school." The dream felt alive within me, fuelled by the laughter and creativity we shared.

Returning to Zwelitsha after the holidays was always exciting. While my love for acting fuelled me, by the time I was eleven years old, I had discovered another passion, one that would change the course of my life. It all began with a simple problem: my dad would leave me with pocket money, but it never lasted the whole month. Rather than complain, I came up with a plan to stretch it and, unknowingly, laid the foundation for my entrepreneurial journey.

Right across our house stood Dambisa General Store, a bustling little shop that sold everything from groceries to snacks. Among the most popular treats were Lemon Delights, crisp, sweet biscuits that every kid my age loved. But not everyone could afford a full packet. I spotted an opportunity.

Using the pocket money my dad left me, I bought a few packets of Lemon Delights and began selling them loose, one biscuit at a time to the neighbourhood kids. Weekends became my prime business hours. I stationed myself right outside Dambisa's store, and soon, my little enterprise began to grow. Demand increased, and I expanded my offerings. I added bompies, chicken heads and feet, and a variety of sweets to my stock. Business was booming, and I was hooked.

This was more than just a way to make money; it was the first flicker of an entrepreneurial spark that would burn brighter with time. I even overheard my dad telling his friends one day that he wished one of his children would take up entrepreneurship. Silently, I made a promise to myself: *It will be me.*

I didn't know it then, but that small business outside Dambisa General Store was more than just a weekend hustle. It was the beginning of a lifelong love affair with entrepreneurship, a calling I was destined to pursue.

In 1988, I found myself moving once again, this time from Zone Eight, Zwelitsha to Phakamisa Township. Phakamisa is located on the outskirts of King William's Town not far from Zwelitsha and is a relatively affluent township compared to Zwelitsha. It was developed as a residential area for professionals, particularly teachers, civil servants, and other middle-class earners. The houses are generally more spacious, with well-maintained yards, giving the township a more suburban feel compared to the densely packed homes in other townships. The streets are lined with rows of homes, some adorned with well-kept gardens, showcasing a sense of pride among residents.

In Phakamisa, I went to live with my dad's uncle, Mr. Minya, whom I called Malume, and his wife, whom I affectionately called Aunty. Both were dedicated educators. Malume taught at Zwelitsha High Primary School, while Aunty worked at Ndzondelelo Higher Primary School. This move marked a necessary start for me after tensions erupted between my Zwelitsha guardians, Nofenishala and Fezile.

Nomhle and Nofenishala were sisters, the daughters of Veleleni Minya, who was in a polygamous marriage to Nelly Botha and Manci. Nofenishala was born of Manci and Nomhle was born of Nelly. She was technically my dad's aunt and had always welcomed me warmly, along with her relatives. For two years, Fezile had embraced me too, but after a big fight erupted, he demanded that those affiliated with Nofenishala leave his house. My father then turned to Mr. Minya, asking him to take me in.

Moving in with my uncle and his family felt like a new beginning. I joined my cousin Vuvu, who was the same age as I was, along with her sister Chuma and brother Mawabo.

It was in this new neighbourhood that I formed a close bond with my classmate from Zwelitsha Higher Primary, Nhose Makwetu, who also hailed from Phakamisa. I admired her love for reading, often borrowing novels from her collection. In no time, we had labelled each other best friends, finding comfort and camaraderie in our shared love of stories and dreams.

In Standard Five (Grade Seven), we were an unstoppable trio, Nhose Makwetu, Babalwa Mabulu, and me. The competition between us was fierce but exhilarating. Nhose was the undisputed number one, her brilliance shining in every subject. Babalwa followed steadily, holding her place at number two with grace and precision. I proudly rounded off the top three, never far behind them, always pushing myself to keep up. Together, we carried the honour of being the pride of our teachers, a trio whose names were always on the lips of every educator when they spoke of excellence.

But life wasn't just about accolades at school. At home, Malume and Aunty kept us grounded. They ruled with iron discipline, homework had to be done, house chores completed without complaint, and excellence was non-negotiable. Aunty, especially, was a force. She reminded me of my grandmother Matilda, stern, beautiful, and not one for easy smiles. Yet, she was the glue of the household, a master in the kitchen. Her meals were a symphony of flavours, and I secretly lived for the moments when she fed us.

Saturdays and Sundays were sacred for her. She never missed preparing a full breakfast. The house would be filled with the warm smell of home-cooked food and always stuffed with food, eggs, bacon, sausages, porridge, and juice. I remember looking forward to my school lunches and our family dinners, knowing that whatever Aunty served, it would taste like a loving masterpiece hidden beneath layers of discipline.

Moving to Phakamisa was a revelation. It was the first time I saw a bathtub, a real bathtub. In the other homes I had lived in, we bathed using water heated in kettles and poured into plastic basins. Bathing in that porcelain tub for the first time felt surreal, almost like stepping into a dream. Soaking myself in warm water in Phakamisa is one of the luxuries that made me begin to imagine the kind of life I wanted for myself.

I became captivated by the families around me. Many of the children in the neighbourhood came from homes where both parents were professionals, teachers, nurses, or government workers. They seemed happier, or at least that's how it looked to me back then. Their houses buzzed with laughter and order, a harmony I longed to replicate. It was so different from the life I had known in eBesuthwini, where homes were often held together by the sheer willpower of single mothers like my grandmother, Matilda.

In Phakamisa, I dared to dream bigger. I remember sitting with my notebook, scribbling out the life I wanted: a home filled with joy, a marriage rooted in love, and four children, two boys and two girls, just like the family of one of our neighbours. Watching that family was like peeking through a window into a life I craved. I wanted the warmth, the completeness, the sense of belonging that radiated from their home.

Phakamisa wasn't just a place, it was the spark that ignited my desire for a life defined by stability and love. There, I quietly promised myself: one day, I would create the life I dreamed of, with a family of my own, built on the foundation of everything I had seen and everything I lacked.

After school and on weekends, I found myself spending more time with the Makwetu family. Unlike many homes in Phakamisa, where traditional family structures prevailed, Nhose's mother, Sis'Nomava, was a single mother who opened her home to her children and their nieces and nephews. It was a warm, bustling environment that felt like a refuge.

The Makwetu girls, especially the older ones, Nobulali, Nosipho and Nomonde, had a deep passion for music. They formed a gospel group called Holy Sisters and were members of a vibrant church, Conquerors Through Christ Ministries, in Zwelitsha. Nhose and Babalwa, both proud members of this charismatic church, invited me to join them. They excitedly spoke of their faith, describing themselves as "born-again Christians." At that moment, I couldn't grasp the distinction between their experience and my own. I diligently read my Bible and prayed my "Our Father Who Art in Heaven," yet I was haunted by what they said about the dangers of not being born again. The thought of hell terrified me, compelling me to consider attending their church.

However, I hesitated, fearful of my uncle, who insisted we uphold our family tradition of attending the Presbyterian Church. One day, while riding in a taxi with Nhose, we passed by Philbert Cinema in Zone Four, where the congregation of Conquerors Through Christ Ministries met. Nhose showed me her pastor, who was playing soccer with some young members in front of their building. I was astonished. Here was a pastor, not isolated in his office or pulpit, but engaging freely with his congregants!

The following Sunday, I concocted a plan to "study" at the Makwetu residence, using it as an excuse to accompany them to church. As I stepped into the building, I was met with a lively atmosphere, unlike anything I had ever experienced. The congregation was large and filled with energy and enthusiasm. A full band of musicians accompanied the vibrant choir known as the worship team. I marvelled at the words of the songs projected on the wall, momentarily believing God had written them there.

The service was a far cry from any church I had attended in Port Elizabeth. The same pastor I had seen playing soccer just days before took the microphone after the worship team finished singing. He introduced himself as Pastor Oscar Nkosi. He started preaching. His words flowed like power from his mouth to my heart, melting away my reservations. I found myself in tears, overwhelmed by an emotional release I hadn't anticipated.

He quoted from Revelation 3:20 and extended an altar call. Compelled by an invisible force, I stepped forward, and with his guidance, I committed my life to the Lord. At that moment, a profound joy enveloped me; I felt free as if a heavy burden had been lifted.

From that day forward, I missed only a few Sundays, cautious of Malume's suspicions. My Bible became a source of strength, and my prayers deepened in sincerity. The Makwetu family hosted Bible studies that enriched my understanding of the Word, guiding me on my newfound journey of faith.

From being the dynamic trio known as the "Clever Trio," Nhose, Babalwa, and I, with our newfound faith, proudly added "saved girls" to our identities. Our church encouraged us to be bold in our beliefs, igniting a radical passion within us to share the message of Jesus at every opportunity. As we spoke with classmates, we witnessed the incredible moment when several learners committed their lives to Christ.

A scripture that fuelled our fervour was Luke 9:26–27: "Whosoever shall be ashamed of me and of my words, of him shall the Son of Man be ashamed, when he shall come in his own glory, and in his Father's, and of the holy angels." It inspired me to take action. I began moving from classroom to classroom, asking teachers for permission to share the good news. While some teachers welcomed our enthusiasm, others saw us as a disturbance.

One particular teacher, Mr. Camngca recognised our potential and invited us to form a Scripture Union (SU) at school. To my surprise and delight, I was soon elected its chairperson. This role became a platform for me to guide my peers in their spiritual journeys, fostering a community where we could grow in our faith together.

As my time in Zwelitsha ended and the school boycotts in Port Elizabeth subsided, I prepared to embark on a new chapter in my life: high school. Nhose, sensing my mix of excitement and apprehension, offered both encouragement and a warning. "When you arrive in Port Elizabeth, let everyone know you're a born-again Christian. Find a charismatic church to call home. And when you're in your new school, join the Student Christian Movement (SCM). Don't forget to pray and read your Bible, Nosiphiwo, so you don't backslide."

I took her words to heart. Leaving Zwelitsha with a clean pass and a ticket to start Grade Eight, I promised myself I would stay true to my faith. True to my word, I preached the message of Jesus to my family and neighbours, leading my sisters and cousins to the Lord. This journey was just the beginning of my commitment to live boldly for Christ, no matter where I found myself.

REFLECTION

Yes, I vividly remember the moment I felt I "found" faith. It was in Zwelitsha, surrounded by friends who radiated a kind of joy and peace I had never known. Their lives were not easy far from it, but their faith in Jesus was unwavering. Through their love and acceptance, I began to see faith not as a distant concept but as a tangible reality. They didn't preach at me, they simply lived their faith, and in doing so, they invited me into it.

That moment of finding faith felt like coming home. It was as if a light had been turned on in a room I didn't even realise was dark. There was a sense of relief, as though I had been carrying a weight I didn't know I was holding, and suddenly, it was lifted. I felt seen, loved, and understood in a way I never had before. It wasn't just an intellectual acceptance of Jesus, it was a heart-deep surrender, a recognition that I was part of something much bigger than myself.

To me, faith is the quiet assurance that there is something greater than myself at work in the universe. Over time, my understanding of faith has evolved from a rigid set of rules and doctrines to a more relational and experiential connection with God. It has become less about having all the answers and more about embracing the mystery, leaning into the unknown, and finding peace in the presence of the Divine.

- What does "faith" mean to you personally? How has your understanding of faith evolved over time?
- Have you ever experienced a moment where you felt like you "found" faith? What did that feel like?

_____

_____

_____

_____

_____

_____

_____

_____

CHAPTER EIGHT

THE PANTIES THAT TOLD A STORY

When my father enrolled me at iThembelihle Comprehensive School, affectionately known as "Tech," in New Brighton, Port Elizabeth, it felt as if I was stepping into a whole new world. The school loomed larger than Zwelitsha Primary, its double-storey red-bricked walls standing proudly against the backdrop of the township. What struck me most was the presence of white teachers, a rarity in our community, adding to the school's unique atmosphere.

Every day, I took a taxi from my father's home to school, a journey tinged with anxiety about getting lost. To ease my fears, my dad introduced me to Thami Magawu, a friendly face already navigating Standard Seven. Thami quickly became my "mom," embracing a big sister role and introducing me to her circle of friends.

As I settled in, I encountered two familiar faces from Zwelitsha. One was Mbulelo Mguzulwa, now in Standard Eight (Grade Ten), who assured me that his home was nearby. When I inquired about Siphokazi, he mentioned she was enrolled at Newell High School, another school nearby. To my delight, I also spotted Thembekazi Gwedashe, a classmate from Zwelitsha, who turned out to be from Port Elizabeth as well. We were reunited in the same Standard Six class, a comforting connection in this new environment.

Our class teacher, Sandra Peter (née Sokutu), was a force to be reckoned with. Her charisma was undeniable, yet her stern orientation for us newbies was clear: "You are not here for boys; you are here to study and make your parents proud."

The beginning of my journey at iThembelihle was promising. I quickly made new friends with Linda and Neneketsang (also called Ausi), becoming my closest companions. As I became more immersed in school life, I discovered that iThembelihle learners were held in high regard in the township. Many viewed the school as a symbol of affluence. I felt a sense of pride in being part of this esteemed institution, ready to embrace the challenges and opportunities that lay ahead.

After school, life unfolded beautifully. Thami, with her entrepreneurial spirit, ran a bustling hair salon from her home, aptly named Thami's Hair Salon. As one of her "kids," I often enjoyed free hairstyling sessions, which felt like a special treat. My curiosity soon got the better of me, and one day I asked Thami to teach me the art of perming hair. Without hesitation, she gladly showed me the ropes, her infectious enthusiasm turning the learning process into a joyful experience.

Thami was a woman of many talents. Not only was she an exceptional hairstylist, but she also dazzled everyone with her modelling prowess. She had an uncanny knack for winning every beauty contest she entered, effortlessly turning heads wherever she went. Inspired by her achievements and my own background in acting from my Zwelitsha days, I found a spark igniting within me to create something meaningful for our community.

Our after-school hours transformed into a hub of creativity and mentorship. Thami and our friend, Nondumiso, took on the roles of mentors, teaching aspiring models, while I led the charge in drama, guiding budding actors. Together, we nurtured the dreams of the youth in our township, fostering an environment where talent and creativity could thrive.

Recognising the growth potential, I decided to merge our passions into a shared platform. With my father's blessing, I hosted an acting and modelling competition at his tavern, branding it "Miss and Mr. Toast" in his honour. Kids from our township eagerly paid a modest entrance fee of ten cents to showcase their talents, and the palpable excitement in the air turned every event into a celebration of youth and creativity.

The joy didn't stop there. Whenever I visited my grandmother's house, I made it a point to extend this initiative, gathering local youth to organise similar competitions at a nearby shack owned by our neighbour.

For the youth in our community, these extracurricular activities provided more than an escape from the challenges of township life. They gave them an outlet for their energy and creativity, keeping them engaged and inspired. They learnt valuable skills, from the discipline of rehearsing lines to the confidence required to walk a runway. For many, these moments were a source of hope, a way to dream beyond the borders of our township, and a reminder that their talents could take them far.

For a while, I stopped sharing my testimony about Jesus, and with that, my prayer life dwindled. At first, whenever thoughts of Nhose crept in, guilt would wash over me, but over time, my conscience grew numb. My friends were all excited with crushes, constantly asking me about mine. Growing up, I had vowed never to have a boyfriend, let alone sleep with a boy after witnessing the chaos that followed my mom's choices in that area. I was determined not to follow in her footsteps.

But as I watched my friends laugh and stroll home with their boyfriends, a yearning began to stir within me, a desire I never expected. The peer pressure was real, and I soon found myself developing feelings for a boy in Standard Ten. When I shared my secret with my friends, they buzzed with excitement, even though we had no idea how he felt about me. His name was Thabile Zantsi. We learnt his name through Ausi's boyfriend, who was in the same class as Thabile.

Then came the day that changed everything. After school, Thabile approached me, his gaze steady and confident. "I'm Thabile Zantsi," he said, "I live in KwaDwesi, and I'm interested in you. If you feel the same, just say yes." At that moment, my heart raced. I felt as if I was standing at the edge of a cliff, unsure of the leap before me.

Caught off guard, I hastily muttered a "yes" and rushed to catch a taxi home. A wave of guilt crashed over me, relentless and overwhelming. I was afraid that my dad or Nowandile would find out what I had just done. My heart raced as I replayed the encounter in my mind, caught between excitement and apprehension, wondering what this newfound connection would mean for me.

THE PANTIES THAT TOLD A STORY

After I said yes to Thabile, the anticipation of the upcoming school dance, dubbed the disco, buzzed in the air. It was set for a Friday night at the school hall, starting at six and wrapping up by nine. "You should definitely come," Thabile urged, his eyes sparkling with enthusiasm. My friends were all going, and even Thami was planning to attend. But when I approached my dad, a frown creased his brow.

"Absolutely not," he said firmly, his tone leaving no room for argument. He went on to lecture me about the risks of nighttime events, emphasising how easily boys could take advantage of unsuspecting girls. It was ironic, really—my father, who owned and ran a tavern, had an intensely protective side when it came to his daughters. If he ever caught a patron looking at us the wrong way, he wouldn't think twice about throwing them out or even banning them from Toast Tavern for good. His overprotectiveness was both frustrating and endearing, a constant reminder of how much he cared.

At home, our living arrangements reflected my father's priorities. House number three was dedicated to family, while number five was reserved for business. We were allowed in number five only when it was our turn to work the counter, peeking through a small window to serve customers during afternoon shifts. Evening hours were off-limits. I pleaded with my dad, tears spilling as I asked Nowandile to intervene. She spoke to him, and after what felt like an eternity, he relented, but with a condition: He would pick me up at eight. With the disco ending at nine, I felt a mix of relief and anxiety.

On the night of the dance, I took a taxi with Thami and her friend, Nozuko Ncanywa, whom I instantly clicked with and remain friends with to this day. When we arrived, the scene was nothing like I had imagined. The school hall was transformed for the evening, dimly lit with colourful disco lights swirling around the room, casting vibrant hues of red, blue, and green that danced across the walls and floor.

Around me, I spotted clusters of students drinking and smoking, their carefree laughter blending with the thumping bass of the music. I stood by the wall, my initial excitement fading fast, replaced by a sinking feeling of regret. The chaotic atmosphere was overwhelming, and my head spun as I wondered why I had even come.

As the night wore on, the energy intensified, with students becoming more daring in their dance moves. The occasional slow song would play, and couples would step into the spotlight, wrapping their arms around each other for a fleeting moment of intimacy amid the energetic chaos.

Then I heard whispers that Thabile was looking for me. A thrill of curiosity and dread ran through me as he motioned me to follow him behind the school hall. "I want to show you something," he said, his voice low and inviting. I was relieved to escape the chaos, craving fresh air. Behind the hall, Thabile leaned in closer, his gaze intense. "Have you ever had a boyfriend before me?" he asked. I shook my head, my heart racing. "No."

He continued, his questions probing deeper. "So you've never slept with a boy?" I felt my cheeks heat up. "No, and I don't plan to." His eyes narrowed slightly, but he pressed on, "What about kissing? Ever kissed a boy?"

"No," I replied, my voice barely above a whisper.

A smirk played at the corners of his lips as he declared, "I'll teach you about different kisses." My heart dropped, an unsettling sensation creeping in as he leaned closer, demonstrating the baby kiss with his soft lips against mine. I felt tense and unsure.

Then he moved on to what he called a "Roman kiss," but the sensation of his tongue pushing into my mouth made my stomach churn. I instinctively pulled back, trying to create distance, but he didn't let up. My discomfort grew into alarm as it dawned on me just how far this situation had spiralled from anything I had anticipated or wanted.

At that moment, a classmate came sprinting around the corner, gasping for breath. "Your dad's at the gate looking for you!" Panic surged through me as the weight of guilt slammed into my chest. I quickly pulled away from Thabile, breaking free from his grip, and hurried back toward the light, my mind spinning.

THE GIFT WITHIN

The car ride home with my dad felt like an eternity. I sat quietly, my heart racing and guilt eating away at me. What if he knew? What if he could see the mess inside me? Shame wrapped around me like a heavy blanket, and I was sure he would somehow figure out what had happened that night.

Not long after that night with Thabile, where I awkwardly learnt about kissing, my period started for the first time. The memory of walking with Sis Nokuzola, Nowandile's younger sister, came rushing back. I had been curious about menstruation after Ausi, my friend, had casually asked me if I had already started. I remember the way her eyes widened when I told her I hadn't and the way she quickly masked her surprise. Feeling embarrassed and left out, I pretended to know what she was talking about.

Later, I gathered the courage to ask Sis Nokuzola about it. She gave me a brief explanation, but what stuck with me was her quick and quiet remark, "It happens to girls with boyfriends." My heart sank. I didn't have a boyfriend at the time, but suddenly, everything made sense. Ausi had a boyfriend, so, of course, she knew about menstruation. It was all connected, or so I thought.

So, when my period finally arrived after that strange, unsettling encounter with Thabile, I felt panic set in. Sis Nokuzola's words rang in my head like a warning bell, a girl with a boyfriend gets her period. My mind twisted the coincidence into something more, proof that I had crossed a line, that I had said yes to a boy, and now I was branded.

I kept it a secret, fearful of what Nowandile would think, afraid my mother or grandmother would somehow know just by looking at me. Even when I visited them at eBesuthwini, I hid it, terrified that if they found out, they'd also discover my secret: I had said yes to a boy, and now my body had betrayed me.

****

"Pule raped Nosiphiwo!"

I was half asleep when Bhut' Maria's voice suddenly cut through the quiet night. His shout came from the room next door, startling me awake. It was a hot summer night, and my sisters, cousins, and I had thrown off our blankets to cool down. In the next room, stacks of beer cases reached the ceiling, stored there for when the tavern ran out of stock.

Our home was always filled with people, relatives from Zwelitsha, my dad's in-laws, and local young men and women who worked at the tavern. There was an unspoken rivalry between the relatives and the workers. My dad, ever the hard worker, had his favourites, those who showed the same diligence as him. Pule was one of those workers. He wasn't the most handsome, and people often made fun of him for his looks, but he was respected for his hard work. Well, respected by most except Bhut' Maria, Nowandile's brother, who despised him.

That night, as we slept, Pule had gone to fetch cases of beer from the storage room next door. Bhut' Maria must have followed him inside. As he passed our room, he caught sight of us girls, blankets pushed aside, our short dresses up as we lay sprawled across the bed. What he saw infuriated him.

I was on my period, something I had been hiding from the elders out of fear. I had no pads, so I improvised with whatever I could find, newspapers, toilet paper, even old rags. My stained panties that night told the story I had been desperately trying to conceal. That's when Bhut' Maria's outburst erupted.

I knew instantly what had happened. He must have seen the blood and assumed the worst, that Pule had raped me. My heart pounded as the house erupted into chaos. My father stormed in, his booming voice demanding answers. Nowandile wasn't far behind, her face tight with concern. Pule was dragged from wherever he had been, his protests falling on deaf ears. "I never went into that room," Pule kept saying, over and over. But Bhut' Maria wasn't backing down. In his mind, the blood was all the proof he needed.

The chaos swirled around me, and I lay frozen, my heart pounding in my chest. I knew what this was. It wasn't rape, no one had touched me. But I also knew that the truth was just as shameful. Bhut' Maria must have mistaken the blood for something else. Then, as if things couldn't get worse, my grandmother, Nomhle, was called to inspect me. She and Nowandile took me to a private room. I burnt with shame as she gently checked me, confirming what I already knew. "She's still a virgin," Nomhle announced, her voice calm but firm. "She's on her menses."

The room fell silent when this was announced. My father's anger shifted from Pule to Bhut' Maria, who stood awkwardly, humiliated by the mistake. Pule, now cleared, slipped out of the house, his dignity barely intact. My father scolded Bhut' Maria for his reckless accusation and left the room, leaving Nowandile and Nomhle to deal with me.

Nowandile sat me down on the edge of the bed, her voice gentle but serious. "Why didn't you tell anyone?" she asked.

I dropped my gaze to the floor, ashamed and unsure how to answer.

She didn't wait for a response. Instead, she gave me a quiet lesson on menstruation, explaining how to take care of myself and the importance of hygiene. "You must be careful," she said softly, "especially around your younger sisters. They don't need to know yet."

Then she handed me a pack of sanitary pads, my first.

Relief washed over me, but so did embarrassment. I had been caught in a lie I didn't know how to tell, hiding a truth I didn't understand. But at that moment, sitting with Nowandile, I felt something else too, freedom. The secret I had been carrying was finally out in the open, and with it, the weight of shame began to lift.

Nowandile hadn't shown me how to use the sanitary towels. I thought I had figured it out, but I was painfully wrong. I stood in the cramped girls' toilet, struggling to peel the pad off, each tug making me wince. "Yho! Why does this thing hurt so much to pull off?" I gasped, fighting back tears as the adhesive clung stubbornly to my pubic hair. Every pull felt like I was tearing myself apart.

Ausi stood by the door, her arms folded, trying to stifle a giggle. "What's wrong?" she asked, her curiosity getting the best of her. When I told her, she burst out laughing. "You put it the wrong way," she said, still chuckling. My heart sank as the realisation hit: I had worn the pad backwards, with the sticky side against my skin.

I wanted to disappear right then and there. But more than the sting of the adhesive, it was the sting of humiliation that I felt the most. That was just one lesson life taught me the hard way. And it wouldn't be the last.

My relationship with Thabile didn't last long after that year. It was like peeling away layers of a false story. I had believed him to be different. Coming from a religious background, he had promised to honour my wish to remain a virgin until marriage. But as the months passed, I started hearing things. Whispers from girls, gossip from friends. My childhood friend Xoliswa asked me one day, her face filled with concern, "What are you doing with that 'Mr. Can We Be Lovers?'" Apparently, that's how he was known among the girls in KwaDwesi. The nickname alone should have been a red flag, but I had been too caught up in the illusion of his promises.

"You're not on contraceptives, right?" he'd ask casually, but his eyes probed deeper, looking for something unsaid. I knew then that he was fishing for an excuse, a reason to push past the boundaries I had drawn. His friends made him feel small, teasing him that I had to be lying and that I was probably sleeping with someone else. His insecurity felt like a shadow that followed us everywhere, darkening everything we had.

What he didn't know, and what I never told him was that after Nowandile told my mother I had started my periods, my mom grabbed my hand and took me to Day Clinic in KwaZakhele. There, without much discussion, she had me start on contraceptives. It wasn't up for debate. She had lived through enough to know the risks, and she was determined to protect me.

If Thabile had found out, I knew what would come next. He'd see it as permission to cross the lines I wasn't ready to cross. The hints had already started creeping into his conversations, remarks about how his friends thought he was a fool for not sleeping with me. The pressure was suffocating.

That was the moment I knew I had to walk away. I ended things with Thabile, shutting the door on a relationship that had turned into something heavy and draining. Years later, when I met Thabile again, he surprised me by expressing his appreciation for the choice I had made. He admitted that, in our youth, he hadn't fully understood the weight of his actions, but looking back, he respected me for standing by my values and not succumbing to the pressure. He acknowledged that neither of us was ready for the consequences that could have followed, and in that moment, I felt a sense of peace, knowing that my decision had been the right one—not just for me, but for both of us.

Through it all, I learned a valuable lesson: the decisions and choices you make today can leave you with scars that will affect you for the rest of your life. Standing firm in your values, even when it's difficult, can save you from regrets that may never fully heal.

In the quiet that followed, I felt a deep sense of clarity. I rededicated my life to Jesus, stepping back onto the path I knew in my heart was meant for me. In doing so, I reclaimed my peace, choosing to honour myself and my faith above all else.

REFLECTION

Writing this chapter was both a deeply personal and cathartic experience for me. It allowed me to revisit a pivotal moment in my life, a time of confusion, fear, and growth and to explore the complex emotions that came with it. The transition from childhood to adolescence is rarely straightforward, and for me, it was marked by secrecy, misunderstanding, and the weight of cultural expectations. I wanted to capture the vulnerability of a young girl navigating her changing body while grappling with societal taboos and familial assumptions. The fear of being misunderstood, the shame of being "found out," and the pressure to conform to outdated beliefs were all part of my reality.

Yet, this chapter is also a testament to resilience. It's about finding strength in the face of judgment and learning to embrace the natural processes of growing up, even when the world around you seems determined to make them feel unnatural.

I hope this story encourages you to reflect on your own experiences of adolescence and the ways in which societal norms shape your understanding of yourself. It's also a call for greater empathy and open communication, especially between adults and young people. So much pain and confusion could be avoided if we created spaces where questions could be asked, stories could be shared, and natural processes like menstruation could be discussed without shame or stigma.

Finally, this chapter is a tribute to every young person who has ever felt alone or misunderstood in their journey to adulthood. You are not alone, and your story matters. May we all strive to build a world where growing up is met with understanding, compassion, and celebration rather than fear and judgment.

- The relative's belief that menstruation starts when a girl says "yes" to a boy reflects cultural myths. How do such beliefs influence young people's perceptions of their bodies and relationships?

- Can you think of other cultural myths or taboos that affect how people view natural processes?

_____

_____

_____

_____

_____

_____

_____

CHAPTER NINE

SACRED CONTRADICTIONS

In the 1990s, a great revival swept across high schools, breathing new life into students through the Student Christian Movement (SCM). Hearts changed in numbers, and friendships blossomed across school boundaries. I had rededicated my life to the Lord, and with SCM came a sense of belonging and purpose. Miss Sokutu, my class teacher, had her sharp eye on me, not just for my grades, but for something deeper she must have seen.

In Standard Six and Standard Seven, I was her top student, claiming first place in both years. She took pride in my achievements but was never one to settle for less than perfection. If I scored ninety-eight per cent, she would whip me, half-teasing, and ask, "Who did you leave the other two per cent for?" She affectionately called me "Qavi," a nickname inspired by Mbulelo Mguzulwa, who once caught me in high spirits, laughing and chatting animatedly with my friends, and exclaimed, "Qavashe!"

As I drew closer to God through SCM, I discovered that Miss Sokutu was also born again. Our bond grew beyond the classroom; she saw potential in me, the kind of teacher who wanted not just academic success but spiritual fulfilment for her learners. One day, she invited me and Nobulali my friend and classmate to her church, the Way of Life Christian Church, in Zwide.

The church wasn't grand, it was a humble shack tucked behind someone's house on Yumata Street. But the love inside that place was overwhelming. It hit me like a warm breeze the moment we walked through the door, reminding me of the love I once felt at Conquerors Through Christ in Zwelitsha. Miss Sokutu introduced us as her daughters from iThembelihle Comprehensive School, and I knew immediately that I was home. The congregation was small, filled mostly with young people, their energy palpable. Even the pastor and elders were in their mid-twenties, and the atmosphere overflowed with a sense of belonging I hadn't realised I was missing.

But life outside the church wasn't as smooth. Things were shifting at home. My grandmother, realising I was old enough to look after myself, asked for me to move back with her in eBesuthwini. She needed someone to help with errands, so I left my father's house and only visited him and Nowandile on weekends and holidays. Meanwhile, my mother drifted in and out of our lives like an unpredictable tide. Her drinking worsened, and her relationship with my grandmother deteriorated.

The rift between them grew deeper when my mother revealed she wanted to become a *sangoma* (a traditional healer). She believed her calling required her to trace her roots back to Giqwa, her father's clan and change her surname to Qubenge accordingly. This did not sit well with Matilda. My grandmother had always dismissed any connection to Sandi, her first husband and my mother's father. She spoke of him with such bitterness that even from the grave, he haunted her thoughts. Anything negative my mother did, my grandmother would say with a sharp tongue, "*Ufuze utata wakho*" (you just like your father). Whether it was my mother's drinking or her poor handwriting, Matilda blamed Sandi. "You've got bad writing, just like him."

Still, my grandmother had no choice but to support my mother's journey. With quiet resignation, she watched as my mother traced her roots to Port Alfred, a town some 150 kilometres from Port Elizabeth. We visited family members scattered between

Port Alfred and Addo, and I saw a side of my mother I'd never witnessed before, soft, loved, and belonging. In those moments, surrounded by her father's people, she looked lighter, as if the weight she had carried her whole life had been lifted. It was as though the missing pieces of her identity were falling into place, and for once, she was at peace.

My mother's journey was not just a search for ancestors; it was a quest to find herself, and I was a witness to it all. My mother's journey into becoming a *sangoma* wasn't an easy one. While some of her aunts and uncles supported her initiation, others, like my grandmother Matilda, refused to budge. I still remember Mha scolding Matilda, insisting she stop resisting my mother's calling. The house became a battleground. My mother had found solace in a Zionist church, the same one I attended as a child when I lived with her and Bheza. Both had once been leaders in that church, and the contrast between their public and private lives always confused me. In church, they were the perfect couple, smiling, polite, and pious, but at home, they fought like two wild animals, leaving me trapped in the chaos of their double lives.

Matilda, on the other hand, was deeply rooted in the Ethiopian Church of Africa, led by Reverend J.M. Masebe. Everyone in our community called it "Kwatat' uMasebe." My grandmother's youngest sister, Makazi uNozipho, had introduced her to the church, and from that day on, she and my aunt wore their spiritual superiority like a banner of devotion. They openly professed to be born-again Christians and refused to attend any family traditional events, denouncing them as unholy. Occasionally, Matilda would compromise, attending certain gatherings during her spiritual lapses. But whenever she felt "revived," she would return to her fiery disapproval of anything linked to ancestors or tradition.

One thing she never neglected was her devotion to the church and her financial contributions to it. A calendar with Reverend Masebe's face staring down at us hung on our wall, year after year. My mother hated that calendar. To her, it was a symbol of everything wrong between them. "The only person you truly revere is Tat'uMasebe!," she'd mock whenever Matilda lectured her against ancestral veneration.

Living with my grandmother meant I was forced to attend her church, even though I never felt like I belonged. The place was packed with people, all of them eager to catch a glimpse of Tata, the revered figure of the congregation. Whenever he entered the church, the atmosphere exploded. People screamed, danced, and stumbled into frenzies of praise, some directed at God, but just as much at him. As children, we were crammed into narrow passages beside our parents, trying not to get trampled by those overtaken by the spirit, rushing forward to "catch his anointing." Staying with my father gave me a much-needed escape from my grandmother's church. But Matilda, determined as ever, encouraged me to join the youth choir. She thought it would "keep me busy," and I reluctantly agreed. It wasn't long before I realised that some of these youth members didn't live by the same values they preached. There were rumours of affairs, and some girls were falling pregnant. Hypocrisy was thick in the air, but I kept my head down.

Matilda herself added to my confusion. Despite all her sermons about righteousness, she smoked in secret. She'd often send me to the nearby café to buy her favourite brand of cigarettes, Lexington. She smoked in secret, hidden away behind closed doors. The moment she heard a knock on the door, especially if it was someone from church, she'd rush to fling open windows and doors, pretending her brother Ndari had just left, leaving behind the scent of tobacco. It was a little dance she performed, hiding her vices behind the mask of spiritual righteousness.

As I grew older and gave my life to the Lord, my spiritual journey took a different path. I began sneaking out to attend my own church, Way of Life. At church we were taught that Christianity was more than just attending services; it was a way of life. It was about showing the fruits of the Spirit in everything you did, a lesson that resonated deeply within me. But this didn't sit well with Matilda when she found out I had chosen my own path. Eventually, though, she relented.

My mother, on the other hand, was less forgiving. She couldn't understand why I refused to follow the traditional route of my ancestors. It was a battle of beliefs, her *sangoma* calling and ancestral rituals against my newfound Christian faith. Our house became a battleground, not just of churches, but of religions and philosophies, each of us fighting for a place to belong in a spiritual war without winners.

Way of Life was more than just a church for me; it was where I found a new family. I invited my siblings and cousins—most of whom I had already led to the Lord after returning from Zwelitsha—to join me. Before long, my cousin Cleo and I formed a gospel duet. We called ourselves the Holy Sisters after the famous Makwetu Sisters Gospel Group. Our popularity quickly grew in church and the SCM circles. Cleo and I signed up to sing at every possible event, passionately sharing our love for gospel music.

Way of Life became home for all of us. I was deeply involved in the worship team, served as an usher, and became part of the intercessors. I was on fire for Jesus. After school, Miss Sokutu would take me to the taxi rank in Korsten not far from Mercantile Hospital, encouraging me with her words, *"Masiyokukhwaza umsindo ozayo"* (Let's go proclaim the good news). I would preach in my school uniform, feeling shy at first, but I quickly gained confidence. With boldness, I would call people to the altar right there in the middle of the busy streets.

Reactions from the crowd varied. Some would listen intently and respond to the call, while others would murmur, "Oh, shame, this child is too young to be preaching." I was fifteen years old at the time. Occasionally, someone would toss coins at me, as if I were a street performer. But these moments only fuelled my passion to share Jesus. I became known for putting my name forward to share the gospel in school assemblies, family gatherings, or even when we were with neighbours. Every moment was an opportunity to preach Christ and Him crucified.

One Sunday after church, something special happened. Mbulelo Makubalo, one of the elders, approached me and invited me to join the Masithandane Lion Life Club in New Brighton. This was one of the Lion Life Christian Youth Clubs led by John van Breda in Port Elizabeth during the late 1980s and 1990s. These clubs were safe havens for young people like me, providing an environment where we could explore our faith, grow as leaders, and engage in community service. We did everything together, sports, music, and outreach programmes, all while being grounded in biblical teachings.

John van Breda played a pivotal role in guiding the youth, organising events, and fostering a sense of belonging. The clubs met in homes and community centres, creating inclusive spaces where we could connect, share experiences, and grow spiritually. Mbulelo, alongside Xola Skosana and Lunga Salamntu, led the Masithandane Lion Life Club, which mainly consisted of young people from Way of Life who lived in New Brighton and surrounding areas.

There was also another Lion Life Club for the youth from Zwide and KwaMagxaki, led by Xolisa Ncoyo, whom Miss Sokutu introduced as her brother on my very first day at church. This club, KwaMagxaki Life Club, had fewer members, and there was a playful rivalry between the two clubs over who was the most vibrant. I visited KwaMagxaki a few times and made friends there too.

One of my most precious memories from those days was the Lion Life camps at Sumcay campsite. These camps were subsidised and accessible, which was a blessing. They created a holistic experience for us, blending spiritual growth with personal development. We'd gather in prayer and worship but also engage in team-building activities, sports, and deep conversations. The camps helped us form lasting friendships and develop life skills that would serve us long after we left the campgrounds.

What stood out to me most about Lion Life was its multiracial nature, something rare and remarkable in those times. We were actively encouraged to form friendships across racial lines, and the camp felt like a small, hopeful microcosm of what South Africa could be. We would hold hands and sing songs envisioning a future without apartheid, our voices rising together in harmony: *"I see a new South Africa, there will be war no more, no more."* It was a space where unity felt possible, even tangible.

During one camp, I became close friends with Debbie, my first white friend. We spent nearly every moment together, laughing, sharing stories, and forming a genuine bond. By the end of the camp, we promised to stay in touch, and we did, through phone calls. Matilda would always beam with excitement, calling me to the landline to talk to my "white friend." It felt like a small but meaningful step toward bridging the divides of our society.

Then, one day I ran into Debbie at the mall. She was with her family, and my heart leapt as I greeted her with the same warmth and enthusiasm we'd shared at camp. But to my dismay, Debbie barely acknowledged me. She offered a cold, dismissive wave before quickly moving on, a stark contrast to the warm, embracing friend I had known. It was a jarring and painful moment, a harsh awakening that shattered my youthful idealism. Despite the connections we'd built within the safe, inclusive space of Lion Life, I realised that outside those boundaries, the racial barriers were still firmly in place especially when family and the outside world came into the picture.

Later in life, I was disheartened to uncover a sobering reality, despite the noble intentions of Lion Life and John van Breda to foster a nurturing environment for young people, their efforts were tangled in the intricate web of apartheid's agenda. Beneath the surface of support and positivity lurked a calculated strategy by the regime to control youth engagement and suppress political activism. Religious organisations, including those I trusted, were subtly co-opted as instruments to advance the government's interests often at the expense of authentic political expression and silencing the voices of young activists yearning for freedom.

But through it all, my passion for Jesus only deepened. While the world didn't change as quickly as I had hoped, I understood that my calling was to remain faithful. I kept preaching, singing, and serving wherever God placed me, knowing that transformation often begins in the heart before it spreads into the world.

My schoolwork began to slip at the height of my passion for church activities, juggling Masithandane Club, SCM, and every possible church engagement. My focus shifted entirely to my faith, and my grades paid the price. At home, things weren't any better. My mother was in and out of *sangoma* initiation schools, wrestling with her own demons, drinking, and disrupting the little peace I needed to study. Chaos seemed to follow her, and eventually, it wrapped itself around me too. I lost my love for books, and a strange laziness settled over me like a heavy fog.

To make matters worse, our school was plagued by a student protest called "go-slow" where attending class became a matter of choice. I remember skipping maths and hanging out in a spot we called "Sun City," a cluster of classes near the school fence. We'd pass time making fun of people walking by, and in response, they'd throw stones at us while we laughed uncontrollably. One day, as we were lounging there, a teacher stormed in with a cane and dragged us back to class.

Mrs. Phillips, our dedicated Maths teacher, hadn't stopped teaching despite the protests. A handful of students continued to engage with her lessons while I, freshly arrived from Sun City, snatched my friend's homework and copied it hurriedly. When Mrs. Phillips checked my work, she paused, stunned. "Where did you get this fancy formula?" she asked, sarcasm dripping from her words. Before I could stutter an excuse, she added with a sigh, "I'm going higher and higher with the syllabus, and you're sinking lower and lower in the mud." The class erupted in laughter, but inside, I felt a deep sense of shame.

At home, my father's business was failing, which strained our relationship even more. I felt neglected as if I was no longer a priority. In frustration, I once confronted him about abandoning me when I was a child, a conversation that cut him deeply. Though I was a Christian, insecurities weighed heavily on me, and I felt burnt out from the relentless demands of both church and life. I began to learn that even within the church, people often show more of their human flaws, "fruits of the flesh" than the spiritual fruits we're taught to uphold.

Our once-loving church was now fractured. Leaders clashed, and members were divided into opposing camps. I found myself in the thick of the conflict, witnessing friends I had prayed with now walking out the door. It was a harsh lesson in human nature, when church splits happen, only a few people manage to remain friendly and kind. Even though we never said it out loud, those of us who stayed behind saw the ones who left as rivals, like soldiers on opposite sides of a battlefield. Faith, which once felt pure and unshakeable, now felt complicated and weighed down by the imperfections of those I had admired.

REFLECTIONS

Devotion is often seen as a virtue, a deep commitment to something greater than ourselves. But what happens when that devotion becomes imbalanced, affecting other essential areas of life? In this chapter, I explored a time when my dedication to the church was so consuming that my academics suffered. While my spiritual life flourished, my grades told a different story. It was a sacred contradiction, one that taught me valuable lessons about balance, priorities, and the true meaning of healthy devotion.

Through this experience, I came to understand that devotion should not mean neglect. Faith, purpose, and calling are essential, but so are growth, education, and well-being. I learned that honouring one commitment does not have to mean sacrificing another. Instead, it requires wisdom, boundaries, and the ability to discern when passion begins to overshadow responsibility.

- Have you ever been so devoted to a cause or community that it negatively impacted other areas of your life (e.g., academics, relationships, self-care)?
- What does healthy devotion look like to you, and how do you balance it with other priorities?
- How can you ensure that your commitment to something meaningful does not come at the cost of other important aspects of your life?
- In what ways can faith and ambition coexist in a way that nurtures both your purpose and your personal development?

_____

_____

_____

_____

_____

_____

_____

CHAPTER TEN

THE X-FACTOR

At Way of Life, we had a vibrant youth group where deep friendships were formed. We walked long distances together, visiting each other's homes, and I felt a sense of belonging. Matilda, however, was not fond of these visits, especially when she came home from work to a house full of young men. We called each other *abazalwana*, and she could never understand why I spent so much time with them. I can still picture her stern look as she'd call me to her room while the brothers laughed and joked loudly in our lounge. She'd ask, "*Nosiphiwo, bahamba nini ababafana?*" (Nosiphiwo, when are these boys leaving my house?). I would return to the jolly crowd in the lounge, pretending all was normal, and discreetly ask them to leave.

Among the brothers who frequented our house was Xolisa Ncoyo, a boy I secretly liked. I never told anyone except my cousin, Cleo, and it became our little secret. At church, dating wasn't encouraged unless, of course, you were planning to get married. But everyone knew that some couples dated in secret. I remember one youth debate we held on the topic of dating, with arguments for and against. To my dismay, Xolisa was fiercely on the *against* side. "When the time is right," he declared passionately, "God will provide a suitable wife." I could have sunk into the floor right there.

Cleo, ever the optimist, would encourage me. "He feels the same way about you," she'd whisper whenever I began to doubt. Her words kept my little flame of hope alive. I even began writing letters to God in my black two-quire notebook. "Dear God," one entry began, "I pray I get married to Xolisa Ncoyo."

The first time I saw Xolisa, there wasn't an instant connection. I remember sitting behind him in the front row at Way of Life, watching him dance, and thinking he reminded me of someone from Conquerors Through Christ Church in Zwelitsha. Over time, though, we grew closer through the youth group, and I became particularly good friends with his sister, Zoliswa. Our bond solidified when we were both chosen as bridesmaids for a church couple's wedding. Cleo also grew fond of the Ncoyos and even started spending nights at their house, strengthening her friendship with Zoliswa.

Whenever Cleo returned from a visit, I would fish for information, anything to suggest that Xolisa had feelings for me. But the boy had a talent for hiding his emotions, and I could never tell.

When Xolisa went through his traditional initiation, I attended his welcome-home celebration. His smile, still radiant beneath the red ochre on his face, made my heart race. But I scolded myself again: *"Get a grip! Stop imagining things."*

One day, as I was lining our bookshelf with old newspapers, my eyes fell on the front page of one issue, and there he was, Xolisa's face staring back at me. He had been named the top matric student for all black schools in the Eastern Cape. Without even thinking, I kissed the picture. Then, catching myself, I pulled back in horror. *What am I doing?* I thought, scolding myself in the name of Jesus for being naughty. From then on, whenever he came to mind, I would rebuke myself, confused whether it was God whispering to me or the devil playing tricks.

When he left for Wits University after recess, our youth group walked him to the bus station. Back at home, I cried hysterically, as if I had lost my closest friend. He promised to write to all of us from Johannesburg, and I lived for those letters. Even though the envelopes were addressed to me, they always began impersonally: "Dear saints in PE…"

Several brothers at church expressed romantic interest in me over the years. One even claimed that God had told him I was meant to be his wife. I shut that down immediately. "That's not God—it's manipulation," I told him. Even at a young age, I knew that God would speak to me directly about matters of my heart.

During the university holidays, Xolisa began visiting me alone. We would sit for hours, talking about everything and nothing. One day, I told him about the brother who insisted God said he must marry me and how the same brother, angry at my rejection, had cursed me, saying no one would ever marry me. Xolisa laughed at the absurdity of it and then, with a seriousness that stopped me cold, he confessed.

He told me that from the very first day his sister introduced us at Way of Life, he knew I was the one. "I remember clearly what God said," he whispered. "You will be my wife." His words stunned me. All those years, I thought I had harboured a one-sided crush, convinced he didn't notice me. But for him, it had been love at first sight.

I dashed to my room, grabbed my black notebook, and showed him the letters I had written to God about him. We sat there, holding the pages between us, marvelling at how our hearts had been aligned all along. That day, we officially became an item, though we kept it a secret from almost everyone, just as the church expected. It was easy to conceal because he was at Wits University in Johannesburg, and I was in Port Elizabeth. We maintained our relationship through long letters and phone calls, sneaking in moments together during holidays, mostly in the company of others, especially Cleo.

Looking back, I realise now that our love was written not just in letters to each other but in prayers, dreams, and divine timing. What began as a friendship grew into something sacred, and through it all, God's hand was guiding us. We just didn't see it at first.

The first person I wanted to tell about my relationship was Nowandile. We were incredibly close. She was my bonus mom in every sense and never treated me like a stepdaughter. For the longest time, I called her "mama" before we nicknamed her "Nowans," a name that stuck for life. I felt even closer to her than to my own biological mother. Nowans was the kind of mom who made life easy, playful and fun but was firm when necessary. My parents Nowandile, Thobile, Matilda, and Nomvuyo each loved me deeply, creating a family dynamic that worked long before the idea of a "blended family" became fashionable. In our world, I was never a "step" anything; I was simply her daughter. Even today, my siblings and I never use the word "stepsisters" because Nowans taught us through words and actions that family is more than titles.

It was beautiful to see how my sister, Thotyelwa, formed a close bond with my biological mother, Nomvuyo. They shared heart-to-heart conversations, especially when my sister had matters of the heart to discuss. Meanwhile, I maintained my unbreakable connection with Nowans.

When I confided in Nowans about Xolisa, she welcomed the news warmly, even though she hadn't met him yet. I think she might have told my dad before I did. Eventually, I told my mom, and though I don't remember telling my grandmother, her body language gave her approval. With a knowing look, she'd casually say, "*Awubambeki xa kukho lomfana mde*" (You seem distracted when that tall boy is around). All my parents gave their silent nods of acceptance, and it filled me with peace.

Xolisa and I would walk far from my home to Swartkops, just to buy Cabana juice and Cornish pies. On those walks, we talked endlessly about our faith, our dreams, and the futures we imagined together. Even back then, I knew without a doubt that I wanted to spend my life with him. When I left to study at PE Technikon (now Nelson Mandela University), our connection remained strong. There were no cellphones in those days, so we kept in touch through public payphones. I would patiently wait for my turn, making space for others to call, then finally take my turn when I could. And we continued writing letters, this time, no longer addressed to saints, but to *Nosiphiwo Mali*. His words were a constant warmth in my heart, and our love only deepened with time.

When Xolisa started working, he sent his family to my house to pay lobola, marking the start of a new chapter rich with family dynamics that tested our blended bonds and traditions. My four parents, my grandmother, my dad, my bonus mother Nowandile, and my biological mother had grown close over the years, forming a quiet alliance built on shared milestones, celebrations, and, of course, challenges. They had learnt, often through trial and error, how to navigate the intersections of love, loyalty, and the inevitable demands of tradition.

But tradition is a strong tide, and ours demanded that *lobola* (bride price) be paid to my grandmother. It meant her family, the Qocwa clan, would lead the negotiations, while my unmarried parents were sidelined. This arrangement stirred old histories to the surface, with certain relatives hoping to revive long-kept grievances, particularly those that had simmered between my father and his kin. Tensions rose as stories resurfaced, and in the midst of it all, I remained firm in one thing: I wanted my dad to be part of every step.

Blended families, especially those formed around a child from an unwed mother, often carry the weight of societal judgment and family tensions yet, when approached with love, mutual respect, and a shared commitment to the well-being of the child, these families can achieve something extraordinary, harmony.

I've lived this reality, and while it hasn't always been easy, I've seen firsthand the beauty that unfolds when these relationships work. Big events, such as weddings, *imigidi*, or initiation celebrations, are where the strength of such a family is truly tested and where its rewards shine brightest.

When everyone sets aside their differences and prioritise the joy of the child, magic happens. During my wedding preparations, I witnessed this dynamic at its best. My grandmother, my mother, my dad, and my stepmother all came together, not as competitors or adversaries, but as a family united by love for me. They planned, debated, and laughed their way through the challenges, each playing their part in ensuring the day was as special as it could be. The benefit of such collaboration is profound: the child—whether a bride, an initiate, or a graduate—feels supported and loved by all facets of their family. It creates a sense of belonging that transcends the boundaries of traditional family roles.

What makes these relationships work is a shared understanding that the child's joy is the ultimate goal. When love and respect become the guiding principles, past hurts can be healed, and walls of resentment can be replaced with bridges of understanding. It's not about erasing the complexities or pretending challenges don't exist; it's about choosing to focus on what truly matters: the child and the joy of their milestone.

For me, that unity culminated in a single, unforgettable image on the morning of 6 December 1997, the day Xolisa and I became one; my grandmother, my mother, my dad, and my bonus mother sitting together, side by side, in the front row on my wedding. That moment wasn't just a testament to their love for me but also to the power of forgiveness, collaboration, and faith in something bigger than ourselves. It was a reminder that when blended families work, they don't just support the child; they redefine the meaning of family itself.

Xolisa and I married young, and though some adults worried whether we were ready to handle the responsibilities of married life, we were confident in our love and secure in God's protection and guidance. We knew there would be challenges, but we believed we were ready for the journey ahead. From that day, our lives became beautifully intertwined in ways I never could have imagined, a magnificent tapestry of love, faith, and shared dreams.

Throughout our marriage, Xolisa has been my unwavering support, a partner in every sense of the word. From the moment our first son, Qhama, was born, I witnessed the depth of his love and commitment. The joy of bringing our baby into the world was immense, but so too were the challenges. As new parents, we faced sleepless nights, the weight of responsibility, and the steep learning curve of nurturing a tiny human. Yet, Xolisa was always by my side, calming my fears with his steady presence.

He took on countless late-night diaper changes and soothed our restless baby while I recovered, showing me that we were in this together.

When our second son, Phaphama, arrived, it was as if our family was woven closer together. The love and laughter multiplied, but so did the demands of our growing household. Xolisa embraced the role of a father with grace and enthusiasm, finding joy in the chaos of family life. He created special moments for the boys, whether it was bedtime stories or weekend adventures, always ensuring they felt cherished and secure. His belief in our family and my dreams was a guiding light, inspiring me to pursue my own aspirations.

Xolisa encouraged me to seize every opportunity I got. He understood the importance of my growth, both personally and professionally. He'd remind me of my strength and capabilities, instilling confidence in me. Our conversations became filled with plans for the future, each word reinforcing our shared dreams and aspirations.

Eventually, my entrepreneurial spirit ignited, and I decided to start my own business. This venture felt like a leap into the unknown, but Xolisa stood steadfastly beside me. He offered insights, helped brainstorm ideas, and even assisted with the logistics when I needed an extra pair of hands.

One night, as the world outside fell into a tranquil hush, Xolisa and I sat together on our bed, the soft glow of a lamp illuminating the pages spread before us. It was our brainstorming session, an intimate space filled with ideas and aspirations as we sought the perfect name for my new consultancy. My mind raced as I reflected on the powerful role of vision in our lives. I had always believed that people must have a vision, a guiding light backed by scripture, "Without vision, people perish." It was a mantra that resonated deep within me, a reminder that to have a purpose is to see the end from the beginning.

As I brainstormed, Helen Keller's words echoed in my thoughts. She had faced unimaginable challenges, losing sight and hearing at just nineteen months old. When asked what was worse than being blind, she said, "The only thing worse than being blind is having sight but no vision." That statement struck a chord with me, underscoring the profound importance of clarity and direction.

With my husband by my side, we tossed around ideas for the name of my consultancy. "What about 'Vision Consulting'?" I suggested, feeling a sense of pride in the simple elegance of the title. But Xolisa raised an eyebrow, thinking aloud, "Why not 'Vision 3 Consulting'? It feels plain, just add a number." I chuckled at his practicality.

In a flash of inspiration, I countered, "What about 'Vision4 Consulting'? After all, we are a family of four!" The words hung in the air, and I could see a spark light up his eyes. It felt right, our family name was woven into the fabric of my new venture, a symbol of unity and support. But more than just our family number, four represented my vision for the business itself. It embodied my aspiration to grow beyond a consultancy to expand into whatever our clients needed and to foster partnerships that would flourish. It was a versatile concept, flexible enough to encompass the many directions I hoped to take.

As we continued to refine the idea, I felt a wave of gratitude wash over me. Not only was he there to help me find the right name, but he was also my steadfast supporter, encouraging me to take the next step. "You should enrol in a business course," he urged gently, recognising that while I had run a hair salon, I needed the foundational skills to navigate this new journey.

Sitting there, surrounded by the warmth of our shared dreams, I realised that this was more than just a name; it was the beginning of a legacy built on love, vision, and the unwavering belief we had in each other. The birth of Vision4 was a testament to our partnership, an emblem of our journey together, hand in hand, as we prepared to embrace the opportunities ahead.

The early years with Xolisa were a balancing act between love and lessons. We came from different worlds; he, grounded in frugality and simplicity; me, familiar with a life where my father's generosity meant I never knew how to "stretch the rand." In his family, a single soda might pass between seven siblings; in mine, each one of us was handed our own, the flavour we chose.

Immediately after our wedding, we were settling into life together in Mthatha. Xolisa had already started his job as an electrical engineer for Eskom, while I waited, still job-hunting. One Saturday, just a few months into our marriage, we set out to the Circus Triangle Shopping Centre for our monthly grocery trip. We joined a queue so long it snaked around the store, a usual scene in this little town where villagers flocked to stock up on necessities. The excitement of being newlyweds was slowly giving way to the reality of bills, budgets, and adjustments. I was restless, still without a job, and feeling the weight of relying on him for everything.

Grocery shopping was meant to be a simple task, yet it was there, under the fluorescent lights of Circus Triangle, that our first true test as a couple unfolded. As we moved forward in line, he leaned in and mentioned we'd forgotten to grab rice. "I'll get it," he said, quickly picking a bag from the shelf. But when I saw the brand, my heart sank. It was the cheapest option, the kind that had stones mixed in and blackened grains and needed to be sifted before it could be cooked. I could almost hear my father's voice in my head: *"Quality matters. Get the best or get nothing."*

"Why this one?" I asked, trying to keep my voice steady, even though a flush of embarrassment rose in me.

I pushed back, insisting on the brand I knew, but he stayed firm, talking about the budget in a steady, calm tone that felt dismissive. It stung, a painful reminder that I was contributing nothing financially to our life. Anger bubbled up, a sense of helplessness and pride, and before I knew it, I'd stormed off, leaving him behind with the trolley.

When he came to find me, his hand resting gently on my shoulder, he explained that it wasn't about undermining my opinion. "It's just a matter of stretching our budget," he said, his eyes soft but resolute. We'd lost our place in line, of course, and now had to wait all over again, our once-bright Saturday swallowed by the monotony of Shoprite's endless aisles and queues.

Later, we laughed about it, but at the time, it didn't feel funny at all. The rice argument was the first of many lessons about compromise, about understanding that neither of us needed to "win" if it meant we were working against each other. Our marriage mentors, the Mbambisas, taught us to see challenges as something to tackle together, to name the problem and not blame the person.

Today, as I sit down to write, Xolisa and I look back on twenty-seven years of marriage, and thirty-two years if we count the years we were just two young people finding our way together. Our lives have been braided together in layers of laughter, arguments, and quiet reconciliations. Our hearts are so intricately intertwined that even in moments when our hands or feet threatened to part ways, they couldn't seem to let go. These years are filled with days that tested us, sometimes to the edge of breaking, yet the love we built has endured through it all. It has outshone every trial, growing stronger with each obstacle we've faced. That is why I call him my X-factor—X taken from his name, but also because he has been the unpredictable, irreplaceable force in my life. He is a force that has turned every challenge into an opportunity for us to grow closer. He is the constant variable in the equation of my life, the one who has always balanced me, even when the numbers didn't add up. In him, I found not just a partner, but the missing piece that made everything else make sense.

REFLECTION

In this chapter, I reflect on the journey of meeting my husband, the man I call my X-factor, the one who changed my life in the most beautiful and unexpected ways. From the early days of our relationship to the moment we exchanged vows, I was blessed with the unwavering support of my stepmother, father, mother, and grandmother. Their presence made our union even more meaningful, anchoring us as we stepped into the unknown world of marriage.

Our early years as a married couple in Mthatha, away from family and friends, came with their share of challenges as we learned to navigate our roles, responsibilities, and the realities of building a life together. Despite the struggles, my husband remained my pillar of strength.

When I took the bold step of starting Vision4, his support was unwavering. He believed in me when I doubted myself, stood by me when things felt uncertain, and became a true partner in both life and purpose.

Together, we welcomed the greatest gifts of our lives, our two sons. Watching my husband embrace fatherhood with such dedication and love made me appreciate him even more. He was not just present, he was deeply hands-on, ensuring that our children grow up in a home filled with love, guidance, and security.

Through love, sacrifice, and shared dreams, we built a life that was far from perfect but filled with meaning.

- How has love (romantic, familial, or platonic) transformed your life or reshaped your priorities?

- Have you ever met someone who felt like your "X-factor" a person who changed your life in unexpected ways? What made them so special?

- In what ways have your relationships been tested, and what helped you overcome those challenges?

- How do you define a *hands-on* partner in parenting, and what impact does it have on a family?

_____

_____

_____

_____

_____

_____

_____

CHAPTER ELEVEN

FROM ADMIN DESK TO TRAINING ROOM

"Nosi, besides owning this salon, what else do you do?" Sis Nox, one of my regular clients, asked as she settled into the chair. Her gaze lingered, curious and probing, while I paused, unsure of how to answer.

When people asked what I did for a living, my response was always tentative. "I own Vision4 Consulting, where I do motivational speaking and training," I'd say nervously, the words tumbling out like a confession. At the time, I believed that anyone who stood in front of an audience without a pulpit was a motivational speaker. Training was still uncharted territory for me, with only my limited experience from my previous employer to draw from. Yet, my heart was already committed to the goal of inspiring others.

After registering my company, I decided to start small but meaningfully—high schools. With nothing but determination and a bit of nerve, I approached principals and asked for a chance to speak to their Grade Eleven students. My mission was clear, to inspire them to focus on their academic futures and make informed life choices. I never hesitated to share my own story, including how I used to bunk Mrs. Phillips' Maths class and the sting of my poor matric results because of bunking. My vulnerability became my strength, showing students that setbacks could be stepping stones.

Word spread quickly. Principals shared information about my talks with others, and soon, invitations began to pour in from schools I hadn't even approached. Through referrals and sheer willpower, I found myself speaking to classrooms of eager faces, pouring my heart out to students I hoped would dare to dream beyond their circumstances. Every talk was voluntary, I wasn't chasing fame or fortune. I was chasing purpose. Those early days lit a fire in me, shaping my journey in ways I couldn't yet imagine.

Little did I know that these humble beginnings would ignite a fire that would shape not only my career but the lives of countless students who dared to dream beyond their circumstances.

Still, when Sis Nox asked, I replied sheepishly, "I also run Vision4 Consulting, where I… do training."

"Training!" she exclaimed, her interest aroused. "What kind of training?"

Caught off guard, I fumbled. In truth, I was still figuring out my niche. Sis Nox seemed to sense my hesitation and jumped in, "Do you do communication skills training?"

Communication skills! I remembered spotting that in one of Sis Buli Boqwana's brochures. Sis Buli, my business mentor, had generously offered me her training manuals whenever I needed them. Grateful for the lifeline, I nodded quickly. "Yes, I do!"

She smiled, her eyes gleaming with opportunity. "I work at the university's Small Business Unit as a director. You must come and see me as we have training opportunities for service providers like you, you might be interested in."

Upon meeting her, she told me about a baking cooperative in KwaZakhele that needed training in communication skills for ten days. She asked me to give me a quote?"

I swallowed, trying to keep my voice steady. "A quote? Per day?" I repeated, stalling for time. The truth was, I had no idea what to charge as the first payment under Vision4 Consulting was a one hundred rands honourarium from one of the schools I gave a motivational talk. Embarrassed, I finally mumbled, "How about… fifty rands an hour?"

She blinked in surprise but asked me to send a formal quotation anyway. That evening, I stayed up late, drafting and faxing over the paperwork. To my amazement, I got the deal! My very first formal contract under Vision4 Consulting. I was over the moon, thrilled for this leap into the unknown, though a nagging doubt whispered that I might have charged too little.

It wasn't until halfway through the project that reality hit. Between developing training materials, printing, and travelling back and forth to KwaZakhele, I hadn't just underquoted, I was losing money. Exhausted and disheartened, I shared my concerns with my husband. He listened patiently before taking my hand and reassuring me with a gentle smile, "Don't worry, love. This is school fees. Consider it your first lesson in business." It was a lesson indeed. And with each mistake, my vision became just a little clearer.

Before starting Vision4 Consulting, I read a book that emphasised the importance of gaining at least five years of work experience before venturing into consultancy. I fell short of that recommended requirement, having formally worked for just three years before opening my salon business. Yet, I unknowingly planted the seeds of my consulting journey during those early years of marriage and work.

Xolisa and I began our married life in Mthatha. I was fresh out of Technikon, armed with a Public and Municipal Administration qualification and eager to find my footing in the professional world. Within three months of settling in Mthatha, I landed my first job, albeit through a stroke of divine providence. Our family friend, Qhayisa Tolobisa, recommended me for a position she had vacated at the Presidential Projects Team (PPT). This initiative, spearheaded by then-Deputy President Thabo Mbeki under Nelson Mandela's administration, aimed to fast-track development in the former Transkei municipalities.

I'll never forget the day of the interview. Nervous yet determined, I walked in and presented myself to the panel. My soon-to-be bosses, Errol Sprigg and Dion Ramoo, admitted they hired me on the spot, not for my experience, which I lacked entirely, but for my confidence and potential. "Experience will come," they assured me.

Errol, a former Mthatha Mayor, led the Local Government Division, and I was to be his Personal Assistant. Stepping into the role was anything but smooth. My colleagues, some of whom had eyed the position, were less than welcoming. I was "Qhayisa's girl," and their disappointment in the appointment of an outsider was palpable. Socially, I was ostracised. Some refused to even return my greetings. Professionally, I was thrown into deep waters. The job required strong administrative and typing skills, neither of which I possessed. I was armed only with my qualification and an unyielding determination to prove myself.

In those lonely months, my work became my refuge. I stayed after hours to polish my typing skills and read documents, immersing myself in their content to understand what I was preparing. Words like "business plans" and "tenders" sparked my curiosity. Minute-taking at team leader meetings became an opportunity to learn, and I soon earned accolades for my precise and insightful notes. As I listened to discussions, I secretly wished to be part of the decision-making rather than an observer.

By the sixth month, my hard work paid off. I was named Employee of the Year, a recognition that came with a 100 per cent salary increase. The transformation from an unsure novice to a recognised team member was exhilarating.

One unforgettable highlight during my time at PPT came in 1998 when the administrative staff were trained by none other than Mercia Smuts, the owner of Mercia Smuts and Associates. She arrived with an air of authority, dressed in a sharp brown suit and carrying a laptop. From the moment she entered the boardroom, I was captivated. Her delivery was commanding, and her presence filled the room.

During the training, Mercia asked us, "Where do you see yourself in five years?" While others aspired to management positions, I boldly declared, "In five years, I want to be like you." My colleagues laughed, but I wasn't joking. At break, I approached Mercia and asked how I could follow in her footsteps. She graciously shared her wisdom and gave me guidance that stuck with me.

Five years later, in 2003, I registered my own consultancy. Today, over two decades later, I find myself doing the very work that inspired me all those years ago.

When my husband relocated to East London and the PPT project concluded, a new opportunity presented itself. Dion Ramoo, who had been seconded to PPT by KPMG, reached out and headhunted me for his team at KPMG. He shared that my unwavering commitment and dedication had left a lasting impression on him. Trusting his instincts during my initial interview, he said, was one of the best decisions he had ever made.

Under Dion's leadership at KPMG, my career took on new dimensions. Dion had a no-nonsense approach to work. "Be proactive," he would say, his tone leaving no room for debate. He couldn't stand idle hands or article clerks claiming there was nothing to do. "Find something to do," he'd say, his voice firm yet encouraging "If there's no work, read legislation. Immerse yourself. Grow." I took his advice to heart. During the quiet moments, I'd dive into the Public Finance Management Act (PFMA), its dense legal jargon becoming oddly fascinating. Dion was spearheading a project that involved interpreting the PFMA for the Eastern Cape Provincial Government, and I found myself assisting in preparing training manuals for facilitators. It was tedious work, but I didn't mind.

Those manuals became my late-night companions. My first son, still an infant, often came to work with me in his pram. When I couldn't complete the printing and binding during office hours, my husband would sit by my side after hours, forgetting his own fatigue as he supported me. Together we printed and bound training materials, readying them for the next day's workshops. It wasn't easy, but it was a testament to the passion and resilience Dion seemed to draw out of me.

Perhaps it was that determination that caught his attention. When Dion started travelling to Bisho to facilitate PFMA workshops for government officials, he brought me along—not as a spectator, but as part of his team. My role was small: handing out training manuals and stationery and watching from the back of the room as senior managers engaged with the material. Yet, something stirred in me. I remember Mercia Smuts, the facilitator who ignited my interest in this field.

Watching Dion and others command the room, I thought, "*One day, that would be me.*"

Then the "one day" arrived much sooner than I expected.

One of the facilitators fell ill, and Dion turned to me. "You've been with me long enough," he said matter-of-factly. "You'll take over tomorrow."

Panic seized me. "I'm not ready," I argued, my voice shaky. "That's too short notice!"

He waved off my protests with his signature confidence. "You can do it."

That night, I barely slept. My reflection in the mirror became my audience as I practised and re-practised, trying to silence the voice in my head whispering, "*What if you fail?*"

When the session began, Dion introduced me to the officials. "This is Nosi," he said, his voice filled with confidence. "She'll be facilitating today." Familiar faces turned to me, their expressions expectant. My knees shook as I walked to the front, clutching my notes as if they were a lifeline. I took a deep breath and started.

Something shifted. The fear that had gripped me all night dissolved as the words began to flow. My voice, steady and clear, filled the room. The PowerPoint slides transitioned seamlessly, each point coming to life as I spoke. It was as if someone else had taken over, guiding me through the session with energy and confidence I didn't know I possessed. By the end, I was no longer trembling; I was soaring. I had found my rhythm, my passion.

Dion beamed. On the drive back to East London, he couldn't stop praising me. "That session is yours now," he declared, his voice brimming with pride. I could tell he felt like a mentor who had just watched his protégé take flight.

That day in Bisho was a turning point. It didn't just launch my career as a facilitator; it awakened a passion that still drives me every time I step in front of an audience. The training bug bit hard, and it never let go.

From the moment I started working at PPT, there was a deep, unshakable belief within me: my destiny was never to work for someone else. It was always clear that I was meant to carve my own path and build something of my own. My husband and I shared the same dream—returning to our hometown, Port Elizabeth, and establishing businesses together. Every year, as we sat down together, our vision for the future was clear: entrepreneurship was in our cards. We'd talk about the businesses we would one day start, the hair salon, the property ventures, and so much more. The possibilities seemed endless.

Beyond his successful career as an electrical engineer, my husband also nurtured his entrepreneurial spirit. He started a branding and printing shop as a side hustle in East London, designing logos for local businesses. One memorable project was for Roundy Kula, a prominent East London business owner. My husband crafted his African restaurant logo with care and precision.

In the quiet moments of our conversations, we would often say, "When we finally make the move to Port Elizabeth, one of us will keep working for a while to hold things down, while the other dives headfirst into the world of business." It was understood that I would be the one to take the leap first, as my husband, the head of our household, carried the heavier financial responsibilities. Though I loved my work at KPMG, I knew deep down that my time there was limited.

Then, as an answer to our prayer, my husband's career took a turn, and he was appointed to a position in Port Elizabeth. Without hesitation, he relocated first, taking our toddler son with him, while my mother and grandmother lovingly cared for him until I could join them. We sold our house, and during that transitional month, I was fortunate to stay with my dear friends, Vuvu Nyamakazi and Kolisa Siqoko, who offered me a safe place to rest and regroup.

Finally, I packed up my life in East London and started anew in Port Elizabeth. With the savings I had carefully accumulated, I opened the doors to Lebone Hair Salon, marking the beginning of my entrepreneurial journey. From that moment on, there was no turning back. Full-time employment was a chapter I had closed for good. The dream I had always carried in my heart was now my reality, and I was ready to step boldly into the future I had always envisioned.

Throughout my career, I've witnessed divine intervention in the most extraordinary ways. The threads of my journey are intricately woven with the generosity and support of people I now call my "destiny helpers." Each one appeared at just the right moment, shifting the course of my life and career in ways I could never have orchestrated on my own.

Take Qhayisa Tolobisa, for instance. It was her recommendation that landed me my first job. Then there was Dion Ramoo, who became my mentor, sharing insights and guiding my early steps. Bulelwa Goqwana was my quiet anchor, offering advice and training materials whenever I needed them. Even Nox, my salon client, played a pivotal role, offering me my first paid training gig.

The serendipity didn't stop there. My cousin, Cikizwa, intentionally referred me to Khaya Ndimba during a conversation on a flight, knowing he was looking for a female facilitator. Trusting her recommendation, Khaya took a chance on me, which led to a long-standing partnership with a significant corporate client.

Then there was Zameka, a young woman I met while living in Mthatha. She became a sister to me, and as an HR executive, she connected me to life-changing corporate clients.

When they say, "It takes a village to raise a child," I can safely say it also takes a village to build a career. My journey is a testimony to the power of community and generosity—starting with my husband, my family, my in-laws, my friends, and even strangers who believed in me.

But if there's one destiny helper whose story still sends shivers down my spine, it's Alfie Wagner. After my first training gig with the university's small business unit, I knew I had miles to go in understanding training and skills development. When Xola Mkontwana, a colleague at the unit, suggested I connect with Cynthia Sibanda, who coordinated training programmes, he mentioned it as an opportunity to enrol in the mandatory assessor and moderator courses for facilitators. I followed his advice. Cynthia suggested I speak to Alfie, who was facilitating assessor training for the university. At the time, the R6,000 cost of assessor training was a figure I couldn't even dream of affording. When I met Alfie, I didn't know it yet, but divine providence was at work.

Years later, as he lay on his deathbed battling cancer, Alfie recounted our first meeting. His booming business had left him overwhelmed, and he had been praying for an associate facilitator. Several people had applied, and some came highly recommended, but he did not believe any of them were suitable until Cynthia introduced me. "I knew immediately you were the one," he said, his voice weak but unwavering.

Alfie became my mentor, taking me under his wing without hesitation. He trained me as an assessor and moderator at no cost and even paid me to co-facilitate with him. He introduced me to the world of skills development, helping me carve out my niche and build my business. Through his networks, I connected with clients who sustained me during some of my darkest times—like when my mother passed away.

Back then, I had just moved from working at home to renting a tiny back office on Albany Road. The space was humble: a desk, a desktop computer, a printer, and a fax machine. I used a nearby internet café to send emails and conduct research. My first admin assistant, Nomangesi Tshikana, was a young woman from church who had volunteered to gain experience, and I eagerly trained her in office duties. We were a team of two, but if you called our office, you'd think you were speaking to a bustling training consultancy. "Vision4 Consulting, Nomangesi speaking. How may I assist you?" she'd answer, not letting the phone ring more than three times. If the call was for me, she'd press the hold button, politely ask the caller to wait, and pass the handset to me—even though I was sitting right beside her. That tiny office was a performance stage, and we played our parts with conviction.

Every morning, I would drop my sons at creche, open the salon, and head to Albany dressed in a sharp suit, hair perfectly done. I believed in looking the part, always ready for the moment a potential client might walk through the door. Slowly, but surely, that discipline paid off. We moved to bigger offices, hired more staff, and gained high-profile clients. Yet, I held fast to the lessons of excellence I'd learnt from KPMG and Dion Ramoo. I became the boss who told her team, "Never be idle. Always be proactive."

Looking back, I see that my professional brand stands as a monument to the generosity of family, friends, mentors, and community. This journey has not been solitary; it's been a symphony of countless hands lifting me, guiding me, and believing in me, even when I didn't yet know how to believe in myself.

REFLECTION

Stepping into the unknown is never easy, especially when you don't feel prepared. When I started my career as a Personal Assistant, I never imagined that one day I would be leading a training session, let alone building a successful consultancy in the field. But sometimes, the people around us see something in us before we do. My boss, without warning, pushed me out of my comfort zone and into the front of a training room. In that moment, fear gripped me, fear of failure, of being unqualified, of not being "enough." Yet, that uncomfortable push became the turning point that changed my career trajectory.

Looking back, I realise that growth often begins with discomfort. Every opportunity I received from unexpected training sessions to mentorship from those who believed in me built the foundation for my business, *Vision4*. The journey wasn't always smooth. Doubts crept in, imposter syndrome whispered that I wasn't capable, and the challenge of starting something from the ground up felt overwhelming. But with each step, I learned that courage isn't about the absence of fear, it's about taking action despite it.

This chapter is a tribute to the people who opened doors for me, sometimes before I even knew I was ready to walk through them.

It's also a remindor that we all need a push sometimes and when it comes, it can redefine our future.

- What fears or challenges did you face when stepping into a new role or industry, and how did you overcome them?
- Have you ever been "pushed" out of your comfort zone by someone who believed in you? How did it change your trajectory?
- Just as others have opened doors for you, how can you create opportunities for someone else to grow?

CHAPTER TWELVE

JUST DO IT

Richard Branson has been one of the greatest influences on my entrepreneurial journey. His books, *Losing My Virginity* and *Screw It, Let's Do It*, opened my eyes to the power of embracing challenges and the limitless potential of a bold mindset. Branson's quote: "If somebody offers you an amazing opportunity but you are not sure you can do it, say yes, then learn how to do it later," resonated with me deeply. That simple yet profound philosophy has shaped my approach to business—say "yes," even when fear whispers otherwise, and trust that you'll figure it out as you go.

This mindset pushed me into territories I never imagined. It urged me to often say "yes" to opportunities even before I fully understood what they entailed. And each time, I discovered new skills and layers to myself.

I remember the first time I took this leap of faith. It came in the form of a phone call from Khaya Ndimba, who had spoken to my cousin about me while they were on a flight. At the time, Khaya was the head of Corporate Affairs for the Eastern Cape Region of South African Breweries (SAB). He was searching for a black female facilitator to train tavern owners on business skills and provide guidance through a business mentorship intervention. I was shocked that I could get the opportunity, considering my lack of experience. This was beyond my usual scope, but Khaya believed I was the right fit. After a brief exchange, he requested my business profile, which, at the time, only included the learnership programmes I facilitated with Alfie and some work with UPE Small Business Unit.

I had no formal enterprise development experience, and the project was centred on an industry I knew little about. My only real connection was my upbringing in a tavern, watching my father at work and learning from him. I included this personal story in my presentation, though it felt like a leap of faith. On the day of the interview, I was consumed by nerves. My hands trembled, and my mind raced. When Khaya casually mentioned that he would be joined by Trudy, the national head of Corporate Affairs at SAB, the anxiety deepened. Her presence only made the situation feel more daunting. The stakes suddenly seemed much higher. My husband and I poured our energy into refining my business profile, determined to highlight my strengths while addressing any gaps.

The presentation unfolded seamlessly, and shortly afterwards, I secured a one-year contract with SAB with the potential for annual renewal. The opportunity changed everything. Just like my previous projects, SAB provided capacity building for trainers, widening my network and exposing me to new horizons. Khaya took a chance on me, and I was determined to exceed his expectations.

For months, I became immersed in training and mentoring tavern owners across the region. The work wasn't glamorous, but it was deeply fulfilling. I connected with many tavern owners, some of whom knew my father. They respected him, and that gave me an unspoken bond with them. My background in the tavern world had become an unexpected asset.

Khaya must have received positive feedback from the tavern owners, because he called again, "Do you know how to develop a business plan?" he asked. My answer, of course, was "yes," even though I had never done it before. I quickly immersed myself in learning how to craft one. Not long after, SAB offered me a second contract to facilitate their Kickstart programme in the Eastern Cape. This was a youth-focused entrepreneurship competition, and my role was to help recruit and select young entrepreneurs and then train them in business skills. We worked through boot camp-style workshops, refined business plans, and set up panels to evaluate ideas and select the best ones, ultimately preparing the regional winners for the national competition. For over five years, I ran the programme, and to my joy, some of the Eastern Cape winners went on to succeed nationally. This partnership with SAB lasted for more than a decade, all because I dared to say "yes" without fully knowing what I was getting into.

As I look back now, I wear many hats—skills development facilitator, assessor, moderator, business mentor, and coach, to name a few. I earned each of these titles through hard work, resilience, and a commitment to always give my best. One of my mentors had once told me, "Nosi, people do business with people they like or love." The core of these words is that relationships matter, and this became my mantra. I worked tirelessly to build genuine relationships with my clients, going above and beyond to show them that I truly cared. It wasn't always easy, and I made mistakes along the way, but the grace to ask for forgiveness and learn from those missteps helped me maintain long-lasting relationships. What I had once seen as just a service I provided became a partnership—a true collaboration. And that's how I built my reputation. The work wasn't always glamorous, but it was incredibly fulfilling. Many of the training interventions were conducted in boardrooms or hotels, but mentorship required me to step outside those sterile settings and into the entrepreneurs' world.

One of the most humbling experiences came when I was mentoring tavern owners, many of whom ran their businesses from their homes. I vividly remember visiting one tavern owner who greeted me with such warmth and excitement. She insisted I sit down while she went to fetch us something to drink. As I settled into the chair, her two-year-old child wandered in, visibly wet from an unchanged nappy, and climbed into my lap.

I gently held the child, feeling his innocent trust, while the tavern owner poured a fizzy drink into a dusty, unwashed glass. The scene stirred memories of my own childhood, of the shack where I grew up, sleeping in a cramped room with my mother's mother-in-law, enveloped by the unpleasant smell of cigarette smoke and the lingering stench of alcohol. Although those moments were tough, they were shaping me for this hard work, something I did not know at the time. They had made me resilient and empathic to connect with people from all walks of life.

The work I did, especially with entrepreneurs in rural areas of the Eastern Cape, was far from glamorous, but it was deeply meaningful. It often meant driving for hours on dusty roads, navigating potholes that tested my patience and my car's suspension, to sit with someone who lived in a one-room shack. Many times, there wasn't even a table to work from, so we'd settle under a tree, papers balanced on laps, ideas flying between us like the whispers of hope they carried. These moments weren't about grand presentations or boardroom applause; they were about human connection and a belief that with the right tools, anyone could succeed.

I remember one man vividly. He lived in a single room, a space so tight his double bed barely fit, leaving no room for chairs. He insisted we sit outside. Under that tree, we worked on his business plan, his vision scrawled out on paper that flapped in the breeze. That same man ran a thriving air conditioning installation business, a far cry from his humble beginnings. Today, he mentors others, planting seeds of success in people's lives that remind him of his own past.

These weren't the polished success stories we often hear about in business circles, but they were raw and real, infused with the grit of determination. I saw it in their eyes, the fire that said, "I can do this." And if, on some days, that fire flickered, I was there to fan the flames.

Some of my proudest memories come from SAB's Kickstart programme, where I watched young men and women entrepreneurs transform. They walked in as uncertain dreamers and left as confident builders of businesses. Some became leaders in their fields, their success stories shared across communities.

Nothing compares to the satisfaction of seeing those I've mentored and trained flourish. Whether it was drivers through the Coca-Cola supplier development programme, SEDA clients starting new businesses, or students from NMU Business School's executive programmes, the joy of watching others succeed became addictive. The work I've done through enterprise development, especially in humble settings, has been more rewarding than I could have ever imagined. As I reflect on my journey, I often think that if I never received those opportunities and never said "yes" to challenges that seemed impossible, I would never have had the chance to witness these transformations.

Amid the thrill of watching lives transform through the enterprise development work I poured my heart into, there was an ache I couldn't ignore. It wasn't loud at first, just a subtle tug in my spirit that grew stronger with every mentorship visit. It wasn't the work itself—I loved standing in front of a room full of eager entrepreneurs, their faces alive with ideas and possibilities. But the contrast I saw between men and women after the training sessions ended left me unsettled. Men would call me with bold updates, voices bursting with pride. They'll tell me they'd cracked deals, networked with executives, or boldly pitched their businesses. They wore their victories, no matter how small, like symbols of achievement. But women—women were different. Hesitation clung to their words like a heavy fog.

"I'm not ready."

"I'm shy."

Their voices would trail off as if they'd already convinced themselves that they had failed before even trying. These women were talented. In the classroom, they sparkled, quick to grasp concepts, sharp with their questions, and brimming with ideas. Yet, in the real world, something invisible but powerful held them back. Their self-doubt broke my heart.

It wasn't just their story, though. It was mine too. I knew that hesitation. That quiet, gnawing voice that whispers, *"You're not enough."* I'd felt it in boardrooms, in meetings where I was the only woman, and in moments when I'd swallowed my bold ideas for fear of being dismissed. Seeing these women falter was like holding a mirror up to my own struggles. The weight of that self-doubt sat heavily in my chest.

Why? Why do we, as women, shrink ourselves? What robs us of our boldness?

I began digging into these questions, not just for them but for me, too. And slowly, the answers began to emerge.

From a young age, we were taught to be agreeable, to be pleasant. Boldness and ambition were things for men. We were raised to be modest, to avoid ruffling feathers or taking up too much space. As I reflected, I realised it wasn't just conditioning.

Rejection felt different for us. Where men shrugged it off, many women—me included—let it fester, internalising every "no" as proof of unworthiness.

Then there was the imposter syndrome, that deceptive shadow that crept into our minds, whispering that our success was a fluke, that we didn't belong. In addition, as a result of the constant juggling of roles, mother, wife, caregiver, and entrepreneur, so many women struggled to push past barriers.

And yet, the world misunderstands us. A man is bold; a woman is aggressive. A man is assertive; a woman is arrogant. Many of us didn't realise that the chain of fear of judgement constrained us. The final blow? The lack of role models. How could we believe in what we had not seen? The world didn't offer enough stories of women like us—bold, brave, unapologetically building empires. Without those examples, it was hard to imagine ourselves in their place.

The more I listened, the more I understood. Their hesitation was mine. Their fears were mine. Their dreams, struggles, and doubts were all mine. But I also knew something else: when women step into their power, they don't just change their own lives—they change the world.

So, I made a promise to myself and them. I would do more than teach business strategies. I would teach courage. I would help them to unlearn the lie that they weren't enough. I would remind them and myself that boldness isn't arrogance, and ambition isn't aggression. And I would show them that their brilliance deserved to shine, not just for their own sake, but for the world waiting to be transformed by their light.

That's when the idea for a women's empowerment initiative was born. Through my organisation, Vision4 Academy, I decided to launch a division dedicated entirely to uplifting women. I named it Vision4 Women. The concept was simple but powerful: create spaces where women could learn from each other's stories, draw strength from shared experiences, and build the confidence to break through barriers.

I envisioned events, workshops, and conferences that would inspire and equip women entrepreneurs. These gatherings would feature trailblazing female leaders who had shattered glass ceilings, sharing their journeys to success and the strategies they used to overcome obstacles. I also wanted to give women a platform to showcase their products and services, offering them the opportunity to sell directly to attendees, who could become their first customers.

The plan wasn't just a dream; it became a movement. Vision4 Women was launched in May 2011, and the response was overwhelming. Women from across sectors—banking, academia, government, and the private sector—rallied behind the initiative. They shared their stories, inspiring others to rise above fear and self-doubt. The events became a lifeline for many female entrepreneurs and those seeking employment, a place where confidence was built, connections were made, and dreams were reignited.

Through Vision4 Women, we have witnessed incredible success stories that continue to inspire and affirm our mission. Women who once struggled to find employment, discovered opportunities by connecting with recruitment leaders through our network. Some launched thriving businesses, while others secured long-standing clients who transformed their ventures. Many even found lifelong friendships that began at our events.

The magic of collaboration became a hallmark of Vision4 Women, with our events gaining immense popularity and often selling out. It was truly uplifting to see women coming together, supporting one another, and changing their lives.

Our impact extended beyond the room. Vision4 Women was invited to partner with TruFM for a remarkable event hosted in East London. Social media, particularly Facebook, became a powerful tool for marketing, drawing women from across provinces to join our events. This digital platform also opened doors to national exposure. I had the privilege of being interviewed on esteemed radio stations like Mhlobo Wenene FM and SA FM, thanks to the generosity of Masanda Peter, who arranged the SA FM interview and facilitated a feature about Vision4 Women in *Move Magazine*.

Our local media also played a pivotal role. The *Herald* newspaper shared our stories with the broader community, keeping our mission alive in the hearts and minds of readers to this day. The ripple effect of Vision4 Women's work continues to grow, proving that when women come together, extraordinary things happen.

The success stories of women, particularly those rooted in the Eastern Cape, always left me yearning for more—more platforms to amplify their voices, more spaces to celebrate their achievements. Cities like Johannesburg, Durban, and Cape Town offered fertile ground for such narratives, but the Eastern Cape often felt like an overlooked corner of the country. This quiet neglect created a void that tugged at me deeply, especially as I witnessed countless women leave for recognition elsewhere—a brain drain that felt personal. I saw the gap and knew it was begging to be filled.

The *Vision4 Women Magazine* idea was born from that yearning. Armed with determination and my unwavering "I can do it" attitude, I partnered with Thembela, a gifted graphic designer and one of my mentees from the SAB Kickstart programme. Together, we envisioned a magazine that would spotlight the stories of local women, inspiring others and proving that greatness could thrive even in the humblest of places. Before the official launch, we proudly unveiled our first at a Vision4 women's event, and each attendee left with a copy filled with inspirational stories of remarkable Eastern Cape women. But that launch edition also became the last. Thembela and I soon realised that our enthusiasm wasn't enough to overcome our lack of experience and limited resources. Yet, even in failure, my desire to spotlight local heroines refused to fade.

Around the same time, I heard whispers of Bay TV's launch a community television station dedicated to telling stories of the Eastern Cape. It would later become Mpuma Kapa TV, airing on DSTV channel 260. My mind raced with possibilities. This could be the platform to bring my vision back to life.

Julie Coetzee was my first thought. I had met her during the SAB Kickstart competition. A brilliant filmmaker, Julie's journey in the programme ended prematurely due to a miscommunication about eligibility. Despite the disappointment, we had built a connection, and her exceptional photography skills made her an invaluable ally. However, her production costs seemed far out of reach for my budding idea.

Then came Motse Mfuleni. Bay TV's chairperson and an old friend from our high school Christian movement days. Motse was someone I knew I could trust. When I shared my vision with him, his support was immediate. Together with the station manager,

Lungile Nduvane, they offered me an incredible lifeline: I could host my show at no cost if I covered production expenses. Then, as if in passing, Motse added, "Why not buy your own equipment and produce your show like Basetsana Kumalo?" That offhand remark became a spark. Could I really own my production?

Excitedly, I shared the idea with my husband. His eyes lit up, and the problem-solver in him sprang to life. He immediately began researching what we needed and found a supplier in the US with high-quality and affordable equipment.

Our trip to New York was both a business mission and an adventure. Before leaving, another idea struck: Why not line up interviews with South African entrepreneurs in the US? With the help of Jongi Klaas, a contact who was working in New York, I met Sibongile Buthelezi a South African-born entrepreneur and visionary behind an elite chauffeur service in New York. I sat down with Sthu Zungu, then President of SA Tourism for North America and Canada. Her journey, from Mtubatuba in KwaZulu-Natal to the global stage, was inspiring. Though corporate policies kept her off-camera, her story was unforgettable. I also interviewed Pearl, my childhood friend living in Washington, DC, and even convinced a young South African woman working in our hotel to share her journey. With our new equipment in hand, my husband took on the roles of cameraman and director, while

I led the interviews. Together, we were an unstoppable duo, chasing a shared dream.

Back home, we established Emambozana Studios, our production company, and assembled a team of passionate individuals led by Busi Ntlabati. Many of them were already part of Bay TV, but their energy and belief in our vision were unmatched. In 2013, *Vision4 Women with Nosi Season 1* talk show was launched. Thirteen powerful episodes aired, each one celebrating the resilience and brilliance of Eastern Cape women. We made history as the first independently produced show on Bay TV.

Three years later, Season Two followed. What started as a scribble on a piece of paper had grown into a vibrant platform. Through *Vision4 Women with Nosi* talk show, untold stories of strength, perseverance, and triumph found the audience they deserved, proving that even the quietest dreams could roar to life.

Another bright idea took root in my mind, a bold vision to celebrate and elevate women who were transforming their communities beyond the confines of profit. And so, the Beyond the Balance Sheet (BTBS) Awards were born, a radiant tribute to women redefining success by weaving purpose into their achievements.

Soon, the BTBS Awards became an electrifying annual affair. Women from across industries—business leaders, educators, and community builders—submitted stories of resilience and triumph. Nominees poured in from every corner of the Eastern Cape; some were put forward by colleagues, others bravely nominating themselves.

Their applications underwent a rigorous selection process, culminating in a glamorous awards night where winners from each category were announced. Among the many categories, we introduced a special honour: the Man of Honour Award, celebrating a man who was making an extraordinary impact on society. To qualify for the BTBS Awards, nominees had to hail from the Eastern Cape, regardless of where they resided.

We also presented Lifetime Achievement Awards, a category that touched my heart deeply. Over three consecutive years, these awards went to remarkable women who had shaped their communities and inspired generations. Each recipient's story left an indelible mark on me.

In its first year, the Lifetime Achievement Award found a deserving home in the hands of Mrs Jumartha Majola. I first met her in my office, accompanied by her colleague Mrs. Kawa. Both women, in their eighties, exuded a quiet strength honed by decades of service. They led Hoza Golden Age, a sanctuary for the elderly in New Brighton. Theirs wasn't just a social club; it was a space where grandmothers and grandfathers wove their wisdom into tangible acts of kindness. They crocheted, beaded, and crafted goods to donate to the needy.

Mrs Majola had heard about the work of Vision4 Women and hoped we could help with their Valentine's Day event for the elderly. Her request resonated deeply with me, evoking memories of my grandmother's selfless dedication to her community. My heart refused to say no. Though Vision4 Women wasn't equipped to offer financial aid, I pledged to make the event a success.

Using social media, I rallied friends to join me. Donations poured in—money, a sound system, decorations, meals, and even musical performances. The joy on the faces of those elders, as they danced and laughed, etched itself into my soul. We organised the event for two consecutive years. Honouring Mrs Majola at the BTBS Awards felt like the perfect culmination of her life's work. At eighty-three, she received the award for her lifetime of service, which included leading Girl Guides and founding a club offering drama, karate, ballroom dancing, and soccer to New Brighton youth. Her life motto, "I promise that I will do my best to do my duty to God and to my country," defined her legacy.

The following year, we celebrated Mrs Nontsikelelo Qwelane, the longest-serving teacher I've ever known. At ninety-three, she was still teaching Geography with an unwavering passion, boasting a 100 per cent pass rate. Born in Engcobo in the Eastern Cape, Mrs Qwelane started teaching at nineteen and dedicated over eighty years to the profession. Her acceptance speech moved us all to tears. "When I mark students' scripts," she said, "I don't see mere papers. I see human beings with great futures." Her words encapsulated her remarkable ability to nurture not just minds but also spirits.

The third Lifetime Achievement Award went to Mrs Laura Mphahlwa, affectionately known as Aunt Laura. When I first encountered Aunt Laura, I was a young administrator working for PPT in Mthatha. Though I didn't fully understand her connection to the projects at the time, her kindness left a lasting impression. She once said to me, "I wish I had your age; I would do so much more," not realising how much she had already achieved.

Years later, Lwando Bantom, a Man of Honour awardee, suggested we honour Aunt Laura. I was elated. Aunt Laura, then eighty-six, accepted the award with the same humility and grace I had known her for. Her contributions to healthcare, education, and community upliftment were legendary. She played a pivotal role in sourcing land and funding for schools, serving as a dedicated member of school governing bodies and so much more. Handing her the award felt like a full-circle moment, a chance to express gratitude for her immense impact.

All three women have since passed on, but their legacies endure, lighting the path for women like me. They are, to me, like the heroines of faith spoken of in scripture, urging us to press forward with courage and conviction. I am deeply grateful that I had the chance to honour them while they were still alive.

Today, many BTBS Award winners continue to transform their communities, embodying the essence of Vision4 Women. This movement remains a beacon of hope, inspiring countless others to dream, lead, and uplift.

REFLECTION

Looking back, so many of the defining moments in my journey happened because I simply said *yes*, even when I wasn't completely sure how things would unfold. I have always believed in acting on my ideas, in daring to step forward before everything feels "perfect." That spirit led me beyond training into building *Vision4 Women*, launching a TV show, and creating *Beyond the Balance Sheet* awards. None of these opportunities came with a roadmap. There were moments of doubt, moments when fear could have paralysed me, but I chose to move forward anyway.

What I've learned is this: Clarity comes with action. Waiting for the perfect moment, for all the details to be in place, often means waiting forever. Sometimes, the only thing standing between us and something extraordinary is the courage to start.

So, I challenge you

- What's the one thing you've been hesitating to start or pursue? What's holding you back, and what would it take for you to "just do it"?

- Think of a time when you took a risk or stepped out of your comfort zone. What did you learn from that experience?

- Have you ever said *yes* to an opportunity that felt bigger than you? How did it change your life or career?
- If you had to take one bold step toward your dream today, what would it be?

_____

_____

_____

_____

_____

_____

_____

_____

_____

CHAPTER THIRTEEN

WHEN THE CHURCH CLOSED IT'S DOORS

Before the glorious moments with Vision4 Women, my personal life took a turn I never anticipated. I experienced rejection and isolation, despite being deeply rooted in my faith.

I gave my life to Christ at the age of thirteen, and throughout my teenage years, I was a proud church girl. I met my husband in church, and our sons, Qhama and Phaphama, were baptised there. For me, the church wasn't just a place of worship. It was home, family, and a foundation for everything I held dear.

Growing up, I was taught that the church family was akin to a real family. Almost all my relationships revolved around the church, sometimes at the expense of connecting with my relatives. As a teenager, I grappled with personal issues rooted in how I was born. I often felt like an outsider in both my mother's and father's worlds. My dad had his own family, and my mom lived her own life. In church, I met and befriended many youths my age who came from backgrounds similar to mine. We were vulnerable to one another and shared similar struggles of growing up without our parents. Church became therapy; we frequented alter calls to be laid hands on and were given space to cry our pain out. As youth, we did not only share our struggles. We shared our hopes and aspirations too, the cars, the types of families we wanted, and the types of houses we wanted to stay in.

We were inseparable, bound by a rhythm of shared faith and friendship. If it wasn't a prayer meeting, it was worship team practice, a youth choir session, or simply us gathering in the homes of young couples who welcomed us with open arms and warm meals. Their generosity turned their houses into sanctuaries, and we—a tightly knit family—found joy, laughter, and belonging in every moment spent together.

The church became my training ground, a place where my potential was nurtured, and my voice found its strength. It shaped my public speaking and leadership abilities, paving the way for me to step into roles of influence. From a youth leader at church to SCM leader at school, and eventually a leader at university, each role deepened my sense of purpose. Through it all, I felt an unwavering call to live a life of impact, rooted in service to God and guided by His purpose for me.

The church was my sanctuary, my perfect haven—until it wasn't. As a young girl, I believed the church was a place of unwavering love, unity, and divine purpose. But as I grew older, I learnt that the church, like any family, was made up of flawed, complex individuals. It was a place where love could run deep but so could hurt, where unity could be preached, but division could fester beneath the surface. And where leadership, if not aligned with humility, could wield a brutal hand against those who dared to question or disagree.

The church where I met and grew up with my husband was more than a place of worship; it was our family. We were young, passionate, and full of dreams. Alongside our friends, we stepped into leadership roles, guiding families, building careers, and nurturing the congregation. But beneath the surface, tensions simmered. What began as a small crack—a disagreement here, a miscommunication there—soon became a gaping wedge. Sides were taken, words were heated, and the church we loved fractured.

My husband and I, along with a handful of others, made the difficult decision to leave. We helped to start a new branch of the church in Mthatha, a place that held special significance for us. It was the church we had attended as newlyweds, where we had built deep friendships and laid the foundation of our marriage. Starting the branch felt like coming home, but it was also a leap of faith into the unknown.

In Port Elizabeth, we started small. I opened the doors of my Vision4 Academy training room, and what began as a gathering of twenty members, mostly from the previous church, quickly grew to forty and beyond with new recruits. We were a church without a pastor, relying on local leaders to rotate preaching duties and reporting back to the senior pastor in the mother church in Mthatha. The senior pastor would sometimes send pastors from Mthatha to preach at our local branch, ensuring we were spiritually guided despite the absence of a permanent pastor. It was a season of uncertainty, but also of hope.

During this time, life threw its hardest punches. My grandmother Matilda had passed away, and soon after, Nowans, my bonus mom, lost her battle with cancer. Nowans's funeral was our first as a church, and it was a moment of both sorrow and unexpected blessing. The mother church in Mthatha sent one of its most dynamic pastors to preach, and his message resonated deeply with the packed hall. After the service, people flocked to us, asking where we worshipped on Sundays. They wanted to be part of what they had experienced that day.

As leaders, we secretly hoped this pastor would be sent to lead our branch in Port Elizabeth. He was a friend from our Mthatha days, someone we trusted and admired. When the senior pastor announced that he would indeed be our new resident pastor, we were overjoyed. His arrival brought a new energy to our church. The congregation grew; the atmosphere was vibrant, and it felt as if we were on the brink of something extraordinary.

But at home, things were different. My husband, always a man of quiet conviction, began to pull back. He had never been one to follow the crowd, and his reluctance to fully embrace the new church's fervour frustrated me. In our previous church, he had twice tried to step down from leadership, feeling that we had lost sight of what truly mattered: impacting our community and focusing on Jesus.

At the time, I didn't fully understand his concerns. I was caught up in the excitement of building the institution, of belonging to something bigger than myself. In this new church, my enthusiasm was sky-high. I volunteered for everything—teaching new members, attending prayer meetings, and leading a cell group. But my husband's absence in some meetings was noticeable. He would make excuses to stay home, and I would cover for him, worried about what others would think. Behind closed doors, our arguments grew louder. I accused him of being disengaged and of not caring about our spiritual lives. But his questions cut deeper than my frustration.

"Babes," he would say calmly, "if we're both at church from Monday to Sunday, who's raising our kids? Do you want them to be raised by the television?" His words stopped me in my tracks. He was right. In my zeal to build the church, I had neglected the very people who mattered most—my family.

One day, I found my husband reading a book that irked me to no end. Its title alone felt like a betrayal: *So You Don't Want to Go to Church Anymore*. I was convinced it was the devil's tool, designed to pull him further away from the church. I laid hands on that book, praying fervently, casting out any demons I believed were influencing him. I told him I hated it, that it had no place in our home.

My husband, ever patient and thoughtful, gently shared his perspective. "Babes," he said, "it seems to me that this new church we've joined isn't all that different from the one we left". Our focus has shifted in ways that concern me. It feels like we've become more invested in the structure and image of the church, the programs, the events, and the numbers rather than the heart of what we're called to do: building the kingdom of God and centring our lives on Jesus." He spoke with love and a desire for reflection, not judgment, and his words lingered in the air, challenging me to consider where our priorities truly lay.

I hated every word he said because deep down, I feared they were true. For months, I resisted the book he suggested, dismissing it outright. "I don't need a book to tell me why I should walk away from church," I replied, my voice tinged with defensiveness. Church had been my anchor, my identity, my safe place for as long as I could remember. The programmes, the services, and the community were all part of the rhythm of my life. I thrived on the busyness of it all and the sense of purpose it gave me. The idea of questioning it felt like stepping into a void, untethered and uncertain. It wasn't just a place of worship; it was a part of who I was. To confront the possibility that something might be amiss felt like unravelling a thread I wasn't ready to pull.

But life has a way of shaking us awake. One quiet evening, I picked up the book. I don't know what compelled me to finally open it, maybe curiosity, maybe desperation, maybe the gentle persistence of my husband's faith in me. It was like staring into a mirror. Page after page reflected the life I was living, a life where I had lost Jesus in the very place I thought I was walking with Him. I realised I had been doing everything for the church, for the ego of belonging to a big, vibrant congregation, and not for the Lord. I had been trying to prove something to those we left behind, to show them we were "making it big."

What I found inside wasn't the attack on the church I had feared, but a tender invitation to something deeper, something both unsettling and liberating. The book became a mirror, reflecting the cracks in my own spiritual journey, and a window, offering a glimpse of a faith I hadn't dared to imagine. It challenged everything I thought I knew about church, community, and what it means to follow Jesus. I began to see how much of my faith had been tied to routines, rituals, and the approval of others. How often had I shown up on Sundays out of obligation rather than joy? How often had I traded grace for rules, relationships for programmes, and intimacy with God for performance?

The book didn't just ask me to question the church; it asked me to question myself. And in that questioning I found freedom. Freedom from the pressure to perform, freedom from the fear of judgment, freedom to simply be—with God, with others, and with myself. But that freedom came at a cost.

It was during this season of reflection that I found myself drawn into a conversation on social media. A friend had shared a post titled, "So You Don't Want to Go to Church Anymore?" Comments poured in—story after story of hurt, disillusionment, and pain experienced within the walls of the church. I couldn't stay silent. I added my voice to the conversation, sharing my own reflections. It was a raw, unfiltered conversation, one that I believed was necessary.

I didn't know it at the time, but a member of our church was watching. They took screenshots of the conversation and shared them with the pastors. I was called into a meeting, accused of sowing division and confusion. My husband was there, along with our zone leader, but the tension was palpable. I was stunned when I found out, not because of what I had said but how it was handled. I stood by every word. No one came to me first. No one asked for context or sought to understand my heart. Instead, my words were weaponised, framed as an attack on the church and its leadership. The fallout was swift. Rumors spread. Whispers of my "rebellion" reached the ears of other church members. Friends I had known for years grew distant. The sense of isolation was crushing.

This conflict coincided with the pre-launch of Vision4 Women in April 2011, a platform I had envisioned through my company, Vision4 Academy. It was a space for businesswomen and professionals to connect, grow, and empower one another, a vision that had been brewing in my heart for years. This launch was meant to be a celebration, a stepping stone toward the official launch in May.

But not everyone saw it that way. To some, Vision4 Women was seen as a threat to the church's existing women's ministry. The timing of the launch, coupled with the tensions surrounding my Facebook comments, only added fuel to the fire.

My husband received a call for a meeting with the pastors, but we couldn't attend due to our work commitments. What happened next felt like a final blow. That evening, a friend called to tell me that a meeting had been held with all the church leaders. The decision? My family and I were excommunicated from the church. The reasons were vague, but the accusations were clear: I had allegedly sworn at the church and pastor on Facebook, and Vision4 Women was seen as a front for starting a rival ministry. The relationship was over. Just like that.

The period from April when we were expelled from church to the launch of Vision4 Women in May 2011 was one of the hardest seasons of my life. Emotions ran high—shock, anger, frustration, betrayal, denial, and fear. I felt as if I was drowning. The launch event, scheduled for 27 May at the Radisson Blu Hotel, was supposed to be a celebration. But instead, it became a battleground. Rumours swirled that people were being discouraged from attending. Tickets that had been pre-ordered were being returned. One woman who had been helping to sell tickets told me people were backing out, saying I had sworn at the pastor on Facebook. My heart sank. I wanted to cancel the event. The weight of it all was too much.

Sleepless nights became my constant companion, a shadow that clung to me no matter how I tried to shake it off. The darkness of those early hours felt heavier, more suffocating as if the world had paused and left me alone with my thoughts. I would wake up, tears streaming down my face, my voice trapped in my throat, unable to form the words of prayer that once came so easily. All I could do was sit in the stillness, wrapped in the faint glow of the television screen, watching gospel music DVDs on repeat.

One song, *Thula Wazi NdinguThixo* by Nobathembu Mabeka, became my anthem, my lifeline. The melody wrapped around me like a warm embrace, and the words—oh, the words—felt like they were written just for me: *"Be Still and Know that I am God."* It was as if God Himself was shouting at me through the music, demanding that I stop fighting, stop struggling, and simply trust Him. But trust? Trust felt like a mountain too steep to climb, a river too wide to cross. It was hard. So hard.

The weight of despair pressed down on me, threatening to crush the dream I had poured my heart into. But then, something extraordinary happened: My team rallied around me like warriors refusing to let the battle be lost. Sandi, my ever-dedicated administrator, pleaded with me, her voice trembling with urgency, "Don't cancel. Not now. Not after everything."

My cousins, Lulama and Unathi, became relentless forces of energy, working day and night to sell tickets, their belief in me unshakable. And then there was Saarah, my Muslim friend, who emerged as an unexpected beacon of light in my darkest hour.

While many of my Christian friends quietly stepped back, Saarah stepped forward. "Didn't you always say you believe in God?" she challenged me, her eyes fierce with conviction. "Why are you losing your faith now? Be strong." Her words were a lifeline, pulling me back from the edge of surrender.

The week of the event was a storm of chaos and doubt. I had promised the Radisson Blu Hotel 200 attendees, but by Tuesday, only forty tickets had been confirmed. The numbers mocked me, and I was ready to throw in the towel, to let the dream dissolve into the shadows of failure. To make matters worse, the church—the very institution I had devoted my life to—seemed intent on undermining me. They scheduled a women's conference on the same weekend as my launch, a move that felt like a knife to my heart. Was it deliberate? I couldn't shake off the thought. But just as I stood on the edge of surrender, God seemed to pause, take a breath, and deliver a miracle I could never have imagined.

It was a gloomy, rainy Wednesday morning, the kind that makes you want to pull the covers over your head and shut out the world. I hadn't slept, my mind full of worry. Work was waiting, and I prepared for another tough day tickets being returned, people still talking about the church rumour, and the fear that all our efforts might fall apart. But as I drove through the grey mist, my phone rang. It was the hosts from Umhlobo Wenene's breakfast show, their voices cheerful and excited. They wanted me to speak on air about Vision4 Women and the upcoming event.

My heart beat fast. This was it. A chance to set the record straight, to share the vision, to breathe life back into what felt like a sinking ship. I pulled over, took a deep breath, and poured my heart out during that live interview. Every word felt like a lifeline, a spark of hope in the storm.

The moment I hung up, my phone buzzed again. This time, it was Sandy, her voice bubbling with excitement. "Gillian McAinsh from *LaFemme* wrote about us!" she exclaimed. *LaFamme* is the women's supplement of the *Herald* newspaper. The article was glowing, a beautiful piece that not only celebrated what we were doing but also invited readers to join us at the launch. I could hardly believe it. By the time I reached the office, the energy had shifted entirely. The phone was ringing off the hook. People from Cape Town, Johannesburg, and everywhere were calling to buy tickets. Some had heard me on Umhlobo Wenene, and others had read about us in *LaFemme*.

The buzz was electric, the kind of momentum we'd been dreaming of. By the end of that Wednesday, the event was sold out. Completely. Fifty people were on standby, pleading for tickets, their voices filled with a desperation that mirrored my own just hours before. The rain outside had turned into a steady rhythm, almost like applause, as I sat at my desk, stunned.

The launch of Vision4 Women on 27 May 2011 at the Radisson Blu Hotel was nothing short of a miracle wrapped in magic. The room buzzed with the energy of women; strong, resilient, and hopeful women who carried within them the same fire I felt burning in my soul. They believed in the vision, not because it was perfect, but because it was real. It was a moment I'll never forget, a moment that marked the beginning of something bigger than I could have imagined.

Today, my life is a story of resilience and grace. The church, with all its beauty and brokenness, remains a part of my story, but I've learnt that faith isn't just about Sunday morning rituals or four walls. It's a heartbeat, a rhythm, a way of living that spills into every corner of our lives. My journey has taught me that even in the moments when rejection cuts deep and pain feels endless, God is there—working, weaving, preparing us for what's next.

I've seen God's hand in my life, even in the toughest moments, shaping me, preparing me, and leading me forward. Faith, I've realised, isn't something you just have—it's something you live. It's a journey that asks us to keep growing, keep questioning, and keep trusting. The church, with all its flaws, is still a place of hope and healing for many. My story isn't about leaving the church; it's about exploring what faith can look like beyond its walls.

Vision4 Women is not a rival to the church; it is an extension of my faith, a tangible expression of the call to love and serve others. It is a testament to the truth that God's work cannot be confined to a building or a programme. It is alive, dynamic, and unfolding in the hearts of those who seek Him and in the actions of those who care for others. Through this vision, I have discovered that faith is not about perfection but about presence—showing up, again and again, even when the road is uncertain.

I'm still walking this path, step by step, trusting that God is with me. I'm not afraid of the unknown anymore because I've learnt that it's often in the uncertain, empty spaces where we find the deepest truths and the greatest freedom. My journey isn't over, but I'm moving forward with hope, knowing I'm never alone.

REFLECTION

Rejection cuts the deepest when it comes from a place you once called home. The church was not just a place of worship for me, it was family, community, and belonging. But in an instant, that sense of security was taken away. A Facebook comment, an honest reflection about the struggles within churches, was twisted into something else. My words were carried to the pastors, and suddenly, I was labeled rebellious. Worse still, *Vision4 Women*, a movement birthed from a desire to uplift and empower, was seen as a threat rather than a calling.

Being cast out was heartbreaking. It shook me, not just emotionally, but spiritually. How could a space that preached love and acceptance so quickly turn into a place of judgment and exclusion? I wrestled with feelings of betrayal, loss, and the overwhelming grief of realising that some relationships were conditional.

But in the midst of that pain, something beautiful happened. I learned that faith is bigger than an institution and that true calling cannot be confined within walls. I found freedom in understanding that rejection does not define worth and that sometimes, losing a place in one space makes room for something greater elsewhere.

Healing was not instant. I had to sit with my pain, process the hurt, and allow God to remind me of who I was beyond the labels others placed on me. I had to learn to forgive, not necessarily to rebuild broken relationships, but to free myself from the weight of resentment. I found solace in the unwavering love of those who stood by me, in the strength of my calling, and in the realisation that my faith was never meant to be confined to four walls.

If you have ever faced rejection from a place you trusted, I want you to know this: You are still worthy. You are still called. And sometimes, the doors that close are the ones that push us toward the greatest version of ourselves.

- Rejection, especially from a community you trusted, can be deeply painful. How have you navigated feelings of isolation or betrayal in your own life?

- What helped you heal?

- Have you ever pursued something you were passionate about, only to have it be misinterpreted by others? How did you handle it?

- Think of a time when rejection turned out to be a redirection in your life. What did you gain from that experience?

_____

_____

_____

_____

_____

_____

CHAPTER FOURTEEN

FROM OUTCAST TO ADVOCATE

The house was quiet, the kind of quiet that wraps around you like a soft blanket, inviting reflection. It was 31 December, and the stillness of the evening was a stark contrast to the lively anticipation of the midnight festivities my sons were undoubtedly enjoying with their friends. My husband had retreated to bed early, leaving me alone at the dining room table, a cup of tea cooling beside me as I let my mind wander through the bittersweet tapestry of 2011.

The year had begun with a heaviness I could barely articulate, but as the months unfolded, it had blossomed into something beautiful, something transformative. Vision4 Women, the initiative I had poured my heart into, had become a beacon of hope for so many. The events we hosted were more than just gatherings; they were lifelines for women who had walked paths similar to mine, women from townships and rural areas who had dared to dream bigger than their circumstances. I basked in the testimonies that poured in, women who had found their voices, built their confidence, and grown their businesses, all because of the connections and empowerment fostered at Vision4 Women. It was a reminder that even in the darkest moments, light could emerge.

One of the brightest moments of the year was our first trip to the United States. Chicago, with its towering skyscrapers and bustling energy, had been a pilgrimage of sorts for me. As the tour bus rolled past the Harpo Studios, where Oprah Winfrey had once filmed her iconic show, I couldn't help but grin like a child. Oprah had been my inspiration since my late teens, a symbol of what was possible when you dared to dream big. Though she had long since left Chicago, just being in the space where her magic had happened filled me with contentment. It was a reminder that dreams, no matter how distant, can take root and flourish.

Our journey continued to Florida; we travelled to Miami, where we cruised past the celebrity homes of Star Island, their opulence a stark contrast to the humble beginnings many of us had come from. We then visited Disneyland. At first, I felt a pang of guilt for not bringing our children, but that guilt melted away when I noticed elderly couples, their faces alight with wonder, exploring the park hand in hand. It was a reminder that the child within us never truly fades; it simply waits for moments like these to be reawakened. Disneyland was more than an amusement park; it was a testament to the power of vision. Walt Disney's dream had outlived him, a legacy that continued to inspire generations. Standing there, I felt a quiet stirring in my heart, a desire to build something that would outlast me, something that would touch lives long after I was gone.

From Florida, then came Washington, DC, where we stood in awe of the White House and the Lincoln Memorial. Standing on the steps where Martin Luther King Jr. had delivered his "I Have a Dream" speech, I felt the weight of history and the power of dreams that had changed the course of a nation.

The trip culminated in a heartfelt reunion with my dear friend Pearl, whom I had known since I was sixteen. She had sparked my desire to visit the US, and seeing her again, now a US citizen with a family of her own, felt like a full-circle moment.

But it was New York City that truly stole my heart. The Brooklyn Bridge, a structure I had admired in countless movies, stood before me in all its grandeur. As I walked across it, the city's skyline stretching out before me, I felt a profound sense of gratitude. It was a seemingly small dream, yet God had made it happen. The Statue of Liberty, Ellis Island, the buzz of Times Square, it was all a whirlwind of wonder that left me and my husband with hearts full to bursting. The US had always felt like a distant fantasy, shaped by the countless hours I'd spent watching American television. To experience it in person was a dream come true, one that we would revisit for three consecutive years.

As I sat at the dining table, reflecting on the year's blessings, a thought began to take shape. Vision4 Women had been a success, but I couldn't shake the feeling that there was more to be done. The events were impactful, but they were just that, events. What happened after the applause faded? What about the young girls in the townships and rural areas, the ones who looked up to us but had no one to guide them? Many of us had moved to the suburbs, leaving behind the communities that had shaped us. Who would inspire the next generation if we didn't step up?

The weight of the world seemed to press down on my shoulders every time I heard another story, another young girl dropping out of school, another life derailed by pregnancy, another dream extinguished before it had a chance to bloom. I sat at countless tables, surrounded by well-meaning voices discussing the problems, yet nothing ever changed. The statistics were numbing, poor matric results, especially in township schools, and girls left to navigate life's challenges without guidance, resources, or hope. It wasn't just disappointing; it was heartbreaking. And I was tired—tired of talking, tired of waiting, tired of watching potential wither away.

The idea came to me like a spark, igniting a fire within. What if Vision4 Women could do more than host events? What if we could create a mentorship programme for young girls, starting with high school learners? What if we could create a ripple effect, where every successful woman who attended our events became a beacon of hope and guidance for a girl who might otherwise never see a path to her dreams? Imagine the impact if each businesswoman, each professional, and each leader in our network committed to mentoring at least one high school girl. These mentors could offer not just advice, but also a window into worlds these girls might never have imagined, careers in STEM, entrepreneurship, arts, politics, and beyond. What if these mentors became role models, showing these girls that their dreams are valid, achievable, and worth fighting for?

My heart swelled with excitement as I tore pages from my black notebook and began to scribble down the vision. The crisp sound of paper separating from its spiral binding echoed in the quiet room, each tear a release of pent-up energy. My pen danced across the pages, ink bleeding into the paper as I scribbled down the vision that had been simmering in my mind.

It was more than an idea; it was a calling, a spark that refused to be ignored.

Recruitment and selection. The idea started with how I was going to recruit and select girls from various township schools. The words flowed effortlessly, each letter a building block for something greater. I could see them already, bright-eyed, determined young women, their potential simmering just beneath the surface, waiting for someone to believe in them. They were the heart of this vision, the reason it all mattered. Leadership workshops. I underlined the phrase twice, my pen pressing hard into the paper. These girls deserved more than just textbooks and exams; they needed tools to navigate a world that often underestimated them. They needed to learn how to lead, not just others but themselves. Confidence, resilience, and vision were the gifts I wanted to give them.

Life skills and career guidance camps. My hand moved faster now, the words spilling out in a chaotic yet purposeful stream. I imagined weekends filled with laughter and learning, workshops where they could explore their passions, and mentors who would guide them toward futures they had only dared to dream of. It wasn't just about careers; it was about showing them that their dreams were valid, that their voices mattered, and that they could shape their own destinies.

In my mind's eye, I also imagined a whirlwind graduation ceremony, not years in the future, but right now, as if time itself had bent to honour their potential. The air buzzed with anticipation, electric with possibility, as a group of bright-eyed girls stepped forward, draped in flowing academic regalia. One by one, they approached the stage, their faces alight with a mix of excitement and wonder. In their hands, they clutched mock certificates, each one boldly inscribed with the title of their future dream careers: Doctor, engineer, artist, CEO, scientist, etc.

This would not just be a ceremony; it would be a spark, a moment frozen in time that whispered to their hearts: "*Your dreams are valid. Your future is real.*" I imagined the impact of that moment, how it might root itself in their minds, growing into unshakable confidence. For these girls, it would be more than a symbolic gesture; it would be a glimpse of what's possible, a reminder that the world is waiting for them to claim their place in it. As they walked away, certificates in hand, I could almost see the seeds of ambition taking root, ready to blossom into the extraordinary futures they had just dared to imagine. This, I thought, would be the heart of the mentorship programme, a celebration of their potential, a promise of what's to come, and a powerful reminder that they are destined for greatness. The idea consumed me, and I couldn't sleep until I had shared it with my husband. His unwavering support only fuelled my determination.

When the new year began, I wasted no time in rallying the allies I needed. Xoliswa Mtulu-Dotwana, my childhood friend, was the first person I approached. Her wisdom and warmth made her the perfect mentor, and I knew she would be instrumental in recruitment and selection. Next was my sister-in-law Nontuthu, a high school educator whose insights would be invaluable in navigating the school system. Finally, I reached out to Gigi, whose experience with Scripture Union had given her deep connections with Life Orientation teachers. Together, we crafted an advert and application forms, and within weeks, schools were on board, mentors had signed up, and the Vision4 Women mentorship programme was born.

The inaugural class of 2012 was welcomed with a ceremony that felt like the beginning of something extraordinary. As I looked into the faces of those young girls, I saw not just their potential but the legacy we were building, one that would outlast us all. Our tagline: "Destined for Greatness" wasn't just a slogan but a promise. A promise to those girls, to ourselves, and to the communities we had come from. It was a reminder that no dream was too small, no vision too distant, and no heart too broken to be mended.

We were born with a gift—a gift from God and a gift to others. This truth is etched into the very essence of who we are, a reminder that our lives, no matter how fraught with challenges, are imbued with purpose and meaning. This resonates deeply in the stories of the girls who joined Vision4 Women, young women whose lives, though shaped by adversity, are undeniable gifts to their families, their communities, and the world.

Their stories were not just tales of hardship but powerful reflections of the resilience that defines South Africa's townships, a resilience born out of systemic inequality, socio-economic battles, and an unrelenting desire for change. These young women carried the weight of their circumstances on their shoulders, but also the dreams of a brighter future in their hearts.

In townships, life is a daily battle. Many households scrape by on irregular incomes, with breadwinners working as domestic helpers, street vendors, or in other informal jobs that offer little stability. Homes are often overcrowded, with multiple generations sharing cramped spaces and limited resources like food, water, and electricity. In some cases, where parents have passed away or are absent, older siblings step into the role of caregivers, juggling the responsibility of raising younger brothers and sisters while trying to stay in school. It's a heavy burden for young shoulders, yet they carry it with quiet determination.

Education, often seen as the key to a brighter future, is a hard-fought battle. Township schools are underfunded and under-resourced, with crumbling infrastructure and a lack of textbooks. For many girls, the dream of finishing school is threatened by teenage pregnancies, financial pressures, or the need to support their families. Even the journey to school can be perilous, with long, unsafe commutes exposing them to harassment and violence. Yet, despite these obstacles, they persist. They show up, not just for themselves, but for the families and communities.

Gender-based violence casts a long shadow over their lives, a painful reminder of the dangers they face simply for being young women. Sexual harassment, abuse, and exploitation are pervasive, and public spaces often feel like minefields. Yet, even in the face of such adversity, there are glimmers of hope. Grandmothers, the unsung heroes of these communities, step in as pillars of strength, offering love, stability, and wisdom despite their own limited resources. Extended family and community members also play a crucial role, creating a network of support that reminds these girls that they are not alone—that they are cherished, that they are gifts.

But the girls of the townships are not defined by their struggles. They are defined by their resilience, their courage, and their refusal to let their circumstances dictate their futures. They dream of becoming doctors, engineers, teachers, and leaders. They are inspired by the sacrifices of the women who came before them, their mothers, grandmothers, and aunts who fought tirelessly to give them a chance at a better life.

Vision4 Women became a beacon of hope for these girls, a place where they could see themselves not as burdens, but as gifts, gifts with the power to transform their own lives and the lives of those around them. The mentorship programme is not just a series of workshops and camps; it is a beacon of hope, a sanctuary of possibility, and a lifeline for young girls who had spent much of their lives feeling invisible in a world that seemed to look right through them.

Through the mentorship programme, we aim to show these girls that their circumstances do not define their potential. Each mentor is carefully paired with a mentee, creating a bond that goes beyond the formalities of the programme. The mentors are women who have walked similar paths, women who have faced adversity but have risen above it. They are living proof that success is possible, no matter where you started.

One of the most profound impacts of the programme is the way it has transformed girls' self-perceptions. Many of them have never been told they were capable of greatness. They have never been encouraged to dream beyond their immediate surroundings. However, through the mentorship programme, they began to see themselves in a new light. They started to believe in their abilities and to envision futures they had never dared to imagine.

The impact of the mentorship programme extended beyond the individual girls. It created a ripple effect that touched their families, schools, and communities. Parents who had once doubted the value of education began to see its importance. Teachers who had written off certain students began to see them in a new light. And the girls themselves became role models for their younger siblings and peers, proving that with the right support, anything is possible.

Through Vision4 Women, I had the profound privilege of walking with these remarkable young women. I witnessed their strength, their determination, and their unwavering belief in the possibility of a brighter future. As I reflect on the impact of the Vision4 Women mentorship programme, I am reminded of the power of mentorship to change lives. It is not just about imparting knowledge or skills; it is about believing in someone when they don't believe in themselves. It is about showing them that they are worthy of love, respect, and success. It is about giving them the tools to dream and the courage to pursue those dreams.

These stories are not just theirs; they are mine, too. They are woven into the fabric of my own journey, a reminder of the environment that shaped me and the people who inspired me to keep pushing forward. My life, intertwined with theirs, is a testament to the belief that even in the face of overwhelming adversity, greatness is possible. It is a story of hope, of resilience, and of the unyielding power of dreams. And it is a story that deserves to be told, not just to inspire, but to remind us all of the incredible potential that lies within every girl who dares to dream.

The Vision4 Women mentorship programme was born out of a deep-seated belief in the potential of every girl to rise above her circumstances. When I launched the programme in 2012, I saw it as a one-year pilot—just a small, heartfelt experiment to see if we could make a difference in the lives of a few girls. Never in my wildest dreams did I imagine it would grow into the movement it is today. I had seen firsthand how mentorship could ignite hope, unlock potential, and transform lives, but I never anticipated the depth and reach it would ultimately have. I never dreamt it would grow into a flame that would burn brightly for over a decade, touching countless lives and creating a ripple effect of change.

Back then, it was just me, my belief, and the little proceeds from my consultancy work. My husband and I dipped into our savings, determined to give the programme a fighting chance. I remember thinking, "Let's just try this for a year. Let's see what happens." But what happened was beyond anything I could have envisioned. Little did I know that one year would become the foundation of something extraordinary.

There were moments when the challenges felt overwhelming. These were times when our own funds dried up and securing funding felt like an insurmountable hurdle, after all, the girls in our programme never paid a fee to participate. Mentors came and left, and challenges seemed endless. I'll admit, there were days when I thought, "Maybe this is as far as it goes. Maybe I've done all I can."

But just when I felt like giving up, a call would come—a teacher from one of our partner schools would reach out, not knowing how much I needed to hear their words: "Nosi, I just wanted to let you know how Vision4 Women mentorship programme has changed the girls selected from our school. They stand out in discipline, punctuality, respect, and academic performance." Those words were like fuel, reigniting my determination to keep going.

There were times when the financial burden felt overwhelming, especially as camps approached. I remember one particular camp where I was at my lowest, unsure how I would cover the costs. The girls were already excited, counting down the days, and I couldn't bear the thought of disappointing them. Miraculously, help arrived—friends, family, and even strangers stepped in, providing exactly what was needed. It was as if God was reminding me that this work was bigger than me, that it was meant to continue.

That same camp ended with a moment that will forever be etched in my heart. As the girls reflected on their experiences, one stood up and said, "Mama uNosi, I don't know what it took you to get us here, or what sacrifices you made, but let me tell you how this camp saved me. It saved me from being sexually abused by a relative. It saved me from running away from home to abuse drugs and alcohol. Thank you." Her words broke me. I sobbed, overwhelmed by the realisation that this programme was not just about mentorship; it was about saving lives, about giving girls a chance to rewrite their stories.

Today, as I reflect on the thirteen years of Vision4 Women mentorship programme, I am filled with immeasurable joy. The programme has grown into a movement, supported by a dedicated board of directors, mentor support committee, mentors, and a network of alumni who return to guide the next generation. We've built partnerships with schools, the public and private sectors, and academic institutions, all united by a shared passion for empowering girls.

Seeing girls thrive in careers of their choice, breaking the cycle of generational poverty, and returning to mentor others is a reward no amount of money could ever match. Every heartache and every setback pales in comparison to the impact we've made. Vision4 Women is a testament to the power of community, the strength of collective effort, and the belief that every girl deserves a chance to shine.

This journey has taught me that even when you have a vision and a gift to change lives, life will test you. It will throw challenges your way, financial struggles, moments of doubt, and seemingly insurmountable obstacles. But in those moments, you must dig deep, hold on to your purpose, and forge forward. Giving up is not an option when lives are at stake, when dreams are being nurtured, and when futures are being transformed.

Looking back, I know that every challenge, every tear, and every moment of doubt was worth it. Because with every girl who rises, every life that is transformed, we are changing the world—one girl at a time. And to anyone with a vision, I say this: Keep going. The road will be tough, but the impact you make will far outweigh the struggles. Forge ahead, stand firm, and never give up.

Because within you lies a gift—one that the world desperately needs. Unwrap it, nurture it, and let it shine.

REFLECTION

Looking back, I see how every twist in my journey, every setback, rejection, and challenge was preparing me for something greater. At the time, I didn't understand why certain doors closed or why I had to walk difficult paths alone. But now, I see the purpose behind the pain. Had I not been an outcast, I may never have become an advocate.

Starting the *Vision4 Women* mentorship programme was my way of giving young girls what I never had, a guide, a voice of encouragement, someone to remind them that they are more than their circumstances. I know what it feels like to doubt yourself, to wonder if you are worthy of more, to dream but not know where to begin. And I also know the power of having someone believe in you. Through this programme, I have watched shy, uncertain girls transform into confident young leaders who embrace their potential. This, without a doubt, is the most meaningful work I have done.

This journey has taught me that our deepest wounds often birth our greatest contributions. What once felt like rejection was actually redirection, leading me to a purpose far bigger than I could have imagined. And so, I leave you with this

Whatever you've been through, whatever you've overcome, know that it wasn't in vain. Your story, your struggles, your lessons, they are all part of the gift you are meant to share with the world. Embrace it. Own it. And most importantly, use it to uplift others.

- What is your gift, and how are you sharing it with the world?
- How can you continue to grow and use it to make a difference?
- Who in your life could benefit from your guidance, encouragement, or mentorship? How can you show up for them?

_____

_____

_____

_____

_____

_____

_____

THE GIFT WITHIN

As I close this chapter, I want to remind you, your story, your experiences, your journey, all hold immense value. Every challenge, every triumph, and every lesson has shaped who you are today. You are here for a reason, and the world needs the unique gift only you can offer. You may not always see it, but the impact you're meant to make is already within you, waiting to unfold. So move forward with confidence, knowing that each step you've taken no matter how small or uncertain has been preparing you for something greater. Your purpose is unfolding, and you are exactly where you need to be.

www.ingramcontent.com/pod-product-compliance
Lightning Source LLC
Chambersburg PA
CBHW021139090426
42740CB00008B/849